THE PERFECT LESSON

Revised and Updated

Third Edition

Jackie Beere Edited by Ian Gilbert

 Independent Thinking Press

Published by

Independent Thinking Press,
Crown Buildings, Bancyfelin, Carmarthen, Wales, SA33 5ND, UK
www.independentthinkingpress.com

Independent Thinking Press is an imprint of Crown House Publishing Ltd.

First edition published in 2010 by Crown House Publishing Ltd
(ISBN 978-184590460-9).

Revised and updated edition published by Independent Thinking Press
(ISBN 978-178135088-1). This edition published 2016.

Thunks are a registered trademark of Independent Thinking Ltd.

Quotes from Ofsted documents used in this publication have
been approved under an Open Government Licence. Please visit
www.nationalarchives.gov.uk/doc/open-government-licence/

British Library Cataloguing-in-Publication Data
A catalogue entry for this book is available
from the British Library.

Print ISBN 978-178135244-1
Mobi ISBN 978-178135245-8
ePub ISBN 978-178135246-5
ePDF ISBN 978-178135247-2

Printed and bound in the UK by
Gomer Press, Llandysul, Ceredigion

This book is dedicated to all the teachers in the world who are making such an amazing difference to so many children. I have the privilege of working with them and seeing their dedication and determination. They are creating our future.

Acknowledgements

One day my daughter Carrie asked me to do a workshop at a conference she was producing called 'Facilitating the Perfect Ofsted Lesson'. She couldn't find anyone else who would do it so, of course, I stepped in. I planned a session based on the latest Ofsted criteria that really focused on how to demonstrate progress in learning. I then tried out my idea on my other daughter, who is a teacher in a challenging school, experiencing constant lesson observations. Lucy used this technique with great success. In fact the inspector said, 'You really nailed the progress in learning.' I want to thank my two daughters for their inspiration, love and support.

I also want to thank my publisher Caroline Lenton who had the idea that this could be made into a book, my husband John who has spent many hours checking the book for me and Ian Gilbert who has worked his magic with encouraging and helpful feedback.

I also want to say a special thank you to Bev at Crown House, who is such a pleasure to work with, and Tom for achieving the impossible in a 'little book'.

Contents

Introduction

Most of the very best teachers have experienced an unsatisfactory judgement at some time in their careers. Learn from it, and it will work as a positive force in your development. Dwell on it, beat yourself up about it, argue about it, and it could be destructive and very demoralising.

Remember, an observation is only a snapshot of your teaching. A collection of these snapshots are put together along with outcome data, work scrutiny and comments from parents, pupils and school leaders, to help Ofsted form a view of the impact a school has on pupil progress. Lessons and teachers will not be given an individual grade but everything observed will contribute to the conclusions drawn.

The aim of this book is to make the snapshot of your teaching look not only outstanding but for it to truly reflect your everyday outstanding teaching.

We all want to do well and impress observers in our lessons. This book is written to help you achieve the very best results you can when an official observer or inspector pays a call. However, the guidance will also help you to develop your teaching techniques and to become the great career teacher you want to be.

The advice is not a prescriptive set of rules, but suggests a model around which you can build your own ideas. Its purpose is to help you deliver a lesson that will demonstrate to any observer that the students in your class are making great progress in their learning, under your supervision. 'Progress' is the magic ingredient required for outstanding lessons.

The advice is easy to apply – no matter what subject you teach or what sort of teacher you are. Many different teachers have successfully implemented the strategies offered here and adapted them to suit their different styles, personalities and classes.

The book begins by offering seven simple steps towards creating the 'perfect' lesson. The following chapters then elaborate on these steps, explaining the key ideas within them in more detail. You can read these straightaway or look them up at a later date if needed.

You don't need the 'wow' factor to deliver an excellent lesson but you do need engaged, enthusiastic and determined students who are driven to make progress because they want to learn. You need to be able to nurture this ethos through having very high expectations for all of your students and by using your expertise to enthuse them about new learning.

You also need to be able to accurately measure and respond to the progress they make in your lesson in order to plan the next phase. Your classes have to make a contribution to the value-added results of your school. Therefore your students need to make progress in their lessons. They must move forward with their learning – and *know* they have. And know how they did it – so that they can do it again next time. Equally, if they haven't made enough progress, they need to know why and how to fix it.

In my experience, students and teachers who understand how learning works best for their particular brain and have nurtured the habits of PLTs (Personal, Learning and Thinking skills) find it far easier to achieve success. This is because such an understanding requires developing a language with which to discuss and reflect on learning and how it works. With the right vocabulary, students and teachers can talk about how learning has worked and, perhaps more importantly, how it has stalled or floundered and what they have learned from that outcome.

An observer or inspector needs to see a learning environment that is challenging learners to exceed beyond their expectations and feel the tangible excitement of brains making connections to new learning. This will only develop and be evident to observers if the advice offered in this book becomes part of your everyday practice and is demonstrated in the students' books and class discussions and in the classroom dynamics, all of which take time to develop. The culture of your classroom will allow any observer to see whether or not good learning takes place every day. You will know when you get this right because you will actually wish every day for someone official to walk through the door and see the fantastic learning going on in your classroom!

'Inspection is primarily about evaluating how well individual children and learners benefit from the education provided by the school or provider. Inspection tests the school's or provider's response to individual needs by observing how well it helps all children and learners to make progress and fulfil their potential.'

Ofsted, *The common inspection framework* (2015): 6

Chapter 1

The perfect lesson in simple stages: meeting the new criteria and delivering progress in learning

Schools cannot be judged as 'outstanding' for overall effectiveness unless the 'quality of teaching, learning and assessment is outstanding.'

Ofsted, *School inspection handbook* (2015): 37

There is no one, magic formula or set structure for the 'perfect' lesson but the steps here will give you some ideas on how to develop your own version of the very best learning experiences for your class.

Step 1. Know what they are looking for

How can you ensure, in the brief time an inspector (or other observer) is in your classroom, that it is clear that your pupils 'typically' make great progress, achieve their full potential and exhibit the attitudes and behaviours of great learners daily?

Sharing the criteria for success is essential for any learning experience. If you (or your students) do not know what they are expected to strive for, how do you (or they) know they have achieved success? So, with this in mind, the Ofsted 2015 grade descriptors for outstanding teaching, learning and assessment are shown below:

Outstanding (1)

- Teachers demonstrate deep knowledge and understanding of the subjects they teach. They use questioning highly effectively and demonstrate understanding of the ways pupils think about subject content. They identify pupils' common misconceptions and act to ensure they are corrected.

- Teachers plan lessons very effectively, making maximum use of lesson time and coordinating lesson resources well. They manage pupils' behaviour highly effectively with clear rules that are consistently enforced.

- Teachers provide adequate time for practice to embed the pupils' knowledge, understanding and skills securely. They introduce subject content progressively and constantly demand more of pupils. Teachers identify and support any pupil who is falling behind, and enable almost all to catch up.

- Teachers check pupils' understanding systematically and effectively in lessons, offering clearly directed and timely support.

- Teachers provide pupils with incisive feedback, in line with the school's assessment policy, about what pupils can do to improve their knowledge, understanding and skills. The pupils use this feedback effectively.

- Teachers set challenging homework, in line with the school's policy and as appropriate for the age and stage of pupils, that consolidates learning, deepens understanding and prepares pupils very well for work to come.

- Teachers embed reading, writing and communication and, where appropriate, mathematics exceptionally well across the curriculum, equipping all pupils with the necessary skills to make progress. For younger children in particular, phonics teaching is highly effective in enabling them to tackle unfamiliar words.

- Teachers are determined that pupils achieve well. They encourage pupils to try hard, recognise their efforts and ensure that pupils take pride in all aspects of their work. Teachers have consistently high expectations of all pupils' attitudes to learning.

- Pupils love the challenge of learning and are resilient to failure. They are curious, interested learners who seek out and use new information to develop, consolidate and deepen their knowledge, understanding and skills. They thrive in lessons and also regularly take up opportunities to learn through extra-curricular activities.

- Pupils are eager to know how to improve their learning. They capitalise on opportunities to use feedback, written or oral, to improve.

- Parents are provided with clear and timely information on how well their child is progressing and how well their child is doing in relation to the standards expected. Parents are given guidance about how to support their child to improve.

- Teachers are quick to challenge stereotypes and the use of derogatory language in lessons and around the school. Resources and teaching strategies reflect and value the diversity of pupils' experiences and provide pupils with a comprehensive understanding of people and communities beyond their immediate experience. Pupils love the challenge of learning.

Ofsted, *School inspection handbook* (2015): 48–49

Inspectors are looking for *typicality* in teaching, not the one-off brilliant lesson. They will check whether or not the lesson they are seeing is typical for the teacher by talking to students and looking at their books. This is a very good reason to make sure that what you are delivering each and every day is helping children progress.

Searching for the 'x' factor: what are the magic ingredients that will make your teaching outstanding and demonstrate the high quality of provision in your school?

Key ingredients for success, based on the descriptors above are:

- All the pupils, particularly those who have the greatest needs, are making rapid and sustained progress.
- Able children experience appropriate opportunities to really challenge themselves and fulfil their potential.
- Teachers have very high expectations of all pupils and enable them to learn exceptionally well across the curriculum and this includes modelling and promoting the core skills of literacy and numeracy in all subjects.
- Teachers are constantly checking understanding, giving powerful feedback and intervening with impact on pupils' progress and learning. Pupils are responding to the feedback given and consequently making more progress.
- Imaginative teaching strategies are used to engage and motivate pupils on a regular basis – not just for observations. This is evidenced by their positive attitude to learning.

Consider these, too, as essential elements of outstanding lessons and spiritual, moral, social and cultural development (SMSC):

- Developing independent and resilient learners.
- Using classroom assistants effectively so that they can help pupils make exceptional progress in your lesson.

▨ Assessment is used as an integral part of developing progress in learning. Children's work will demonstrate this and show how they respond to feedback.

▨ Challenging the most able learners to work at full capacity.

▨ Using technology to make an impact on learning.

▨ Effective collaborative learning and peer review.

▨ Effective classroom management to create behaviour and attitudes that really enhance learning for everyone.

▨ Sharing the criteria for success to enable pupils to have ownership of and commitment to their own learning.

So, how can you make sure that you demonstrate the above when being observed or inspected? Practice! You need to be relentless in your efforts to improve achievement for all. Establishing a culture in your classroom where learning is valued and expectations of self and others are habitual and high will mean that anyone walking into your classroom will immediately know that you are a very effective teacher. The following chapters will give you much more detail on how to do this. However, first consider the remaining steps towards the 'perfect' lesson and then dip into the other chapters as you need them.

Make sure that your pupils know that observers may come into lessons to see how they are learning and that they should feel free to chat about what happens in your classroom – they are the best advocates of your teaching and will be keen to explain how you help them!

Step 2. Be present and in control, right from the start

Set up the learning environment

The relationships you have with your students are the most important aspect of setting up your learning environment. You need to be the very best learner in the class and demonstrate this by displaying that same thirst for knowledge and love of learning that inspectors expect to see from the pupils.

> 'Pupils are confident, self-assured learners. Their excellent attitudes to learning have a strong, positive impact on their progress.'
>
> Ofsted, *School inspection handbook* (2015): 52

Students should expect to start work as soon as they come into the classroom, without you directing them. This strategy should cover the time it takes for all the students to arrive. It neatly shows how you are completely and effortlessly in control and makes a great impression on that extra (Ofsted) visitor.

Always make a prompt start – especially for early arrivers. Get the students into the habit of self-starting in every lesson by setting little challenges, questions or tasks on the board that they *know* they are expected to get on with. These can be anagrams, puzzles, true or false statements, recaps of the previous lesson(s), unexpected questions for debate, music challenges and so on. Reward effort for these tasks as part of your reward-and-sanction classroom policy.

It is a good idea to have music on as students come in and are getting on with these tasks (see Nina Jackson's *The Little Book of Music for the Classroom* for some suggestions). Then, when you switch the music off the students know it is time for the lesson proper to start.

While the students are completing the tasks, circulate, smile, greet them individually by name and make them feel welcome. You could get the students to assess each other's work, if appropriate.

This will mean that you can start the main part of the lesson when *you* are ready and useful work is already taking place. It will be obvious to any observer that your pupils are in the habit of starting learning as soon as they walk through your classroom door.

Outstanding *behaviour for learning* requires an exceptionally positive climate in the classroom where all the pupils want to learn, ask questions and support each other unconditionally in making great progress.

Step 3. The starter that primes them for learning

Your first learning activity should stimulate curiosity and open-mindedness and prepare the brain for learning. This can be random or linked to the subject.

> Engaging the emotional brain makes your class curious and attentive.

A starter can be a Thunk, a curiosity or a challenge of some sort.

A Thunk

This is a question (from Ian Gilbert's *The Little Book of Thunks*) that has no right or wrong answer but which makes you think. They prepare students to be open-minded and consider various options. For example:

- If you always got what you wished for would you always be happy?
- Can you point to where the sky begins?
- What has the most freedom – an ant or a school child?
- Is a person who has a face transplant still the same person?
- Which is heavier, an inflated or deflated balloon?

Students can think of the next question or make up their own Thunks as part of the starter.

A curiosity

For example:

- A box – students have to guess what the contents are.
- A wig or hat – someone can try it on and guess the character it belongs to.
- A message in a bottle – students have to guess the message and who sent it.

A creative challenge in pairs

For example:

- What was the first pop song you ever heard and the one you heard most recently?
- What are the three most popular babies' names today and which three will be most popular in 2020?
- Guess the most common and least common food that everyone in the class had for breakfast.

Work for, party with or send to the jungle

A fun task that helps students understand personal preferences. Which would you do with the following famous names and why?

For example:

- Prince William, Jo Whiley, Russell Brand
- Cheryl Cole, Davina McCall, Fern Britton
- Dale Winton, Boris Johnson, David Cameron

> Be energetic and enthusiastic.
> Channel any nerves into passion!

Room 101

This is the room full of your worst nightmare. For Winston in George Orwell's *1984* it was rats. What three things would you put in Room 101 and why?

SMSC development in a school can be an important aspect of the decision about whether a school *is outstanding*. So in your lesson ensure that your pupils are developing the 'skills and attitudes to enable them to participate fully in and contribute positively to life in modern Britain' (Ofsted, *School inspection handbook* (2015): 34) and reflecting on their values and beliefs. Prime the learners in this by linking the lesson explicitly to one of the Personal, Learning and Thinking skills (PLTs) which were identified as the key skills employers require for the workplace. Success could earn points that accumulate over time and gain rewards. Some examples of tasks involving the PLTs appear in the table overleaf.

Personal, Learning and Thinking skills	Task
Self-manager	Draw a face that depicts the different moods you have experienced today so far
Effective participator	Write down five things you will do in this lesson to help others learn
Creative thinker	Design a logo and slogan for this subject/lesson
Reflective learner	Create a mind map of what we did last lesson
Independent enquirer	Write three questions you need to ask about what we did last lesson
Teamworker	Think of three promises you will make to your team to help it work well

Step 4. Set objectives or learning outcomes: engage them in the learning

There is no need for a lengthy typed lesson plan but you do need to plan what you want to teach them and how you will know if you have succeeded!

> **Top tip:** Know your pupils and the context of their achievement in your school. That means knowing which groups need challenging, supporting or pushing (groups which Ofsted are particularly interested in are listed in *The common inspection framework*, pp. 6–7). Inspectors will be particularly concerned about how you are helping those children who show up on your school data as *not* making enough progress, especially with English and maths skills.

Describe simply and *exactly* what you want the students to be able to do or know by the end of the lesson. If you need to, do this with two levels (at least) for differentiation but have high expectations of all students. If in doubt teach to the top and intervene, anticipate and scaffold for those who need it.

Setting high expectations is the single most important thing you can do to ensure good progress in learning. Make sure specific groups of students are aware of what they need to do to make progress. Create a culture in your classroom where all students are willing to push themselves outside of their comfort zone so that they can 'grow' their brains.

This is the crucial moment when you engage the students in the exciting task ahead and explain that it will make a difference to them personally. To succeed you must communicate your expectation of success and your personal excitement about the subject – what they can achieve and why it is important. Ensure that students with particular needs (the most able, the least able, particular ethnic minorities, girls, boys or vulnerable students) have that extra bit of attention, resources or scaffolding to ensure that they know how to make progress.

Doing this effectively shows that you and the other adults are acutely aware of the pupils' capabilities and of their prior learning and that you plan very effectively to build on these. It is even better if your pupils are able to coach each other and themselves because they are aware of how they learn, and how important it is to keep trying, even when they get stuck or make mistakes. If you can develop this habit of resilience in your lessons, it will shine through in every conversation an inspector may have with your pupils!

> Setting up learning outcomes that connect with students
> and their world is crucial to a successful lesson.

How can you convince the students that learning is a journey and that they have an amazing capacity to progress during this lesson? There are three steps to doing this:

1. Explaining (with passion) what success in achieving the objectives will look like and feel like (i.e. the 'brilliant outcome' or WAGOLL – what a good one looks like).

2. Showing them that achieving the objectives is part of a learning journey towards a greater goal by using a continuum line (see the diagram on page 21).

3. By setting one or more personal skills objectives for individual (or targeted) students (see the boxes in the diagram on page 21).

Draw a continuum line that leads to the 'brilliant outcome' they are heading towards in their learning journey. At the start of the activity students should decide where they are along the line. After the task they then mark where they are now to demonstrate what (if any) progress they have made in the lesson towards the outcome. The same can be done for the PLTs which will help the students towards self-assessment of particular skills. These are just as crucial for an outstanding lesson. By including the wandering line you can discuss what the challenges of the task may be, when they may get stuck and what strategies they could use to get 'unstuck'. This is a great opportunity to emphasise that learning is hardly ever a simple continuum but you can expect hard bits which might be frustrating, challenging but if you have the right attitude and strategies you can overcome anything!

We need to ensure that our students develop deep, lasting learning and a set of life skills that will more effectively equip them for the real world.

See the example shown opposite.

A huge arrow across your classroom wall will enable you to talk to the whole class about how they have progressed in the lesson. By using sticky notes you can show their progress along their learning journey.

Learning isn't linear, but as long as we are moving along towards our learning goals, we can become more aware of the process of learning and the cognitive connections required. Research has found that such a focus can make a profound difference on progress (Wall et al. 2011).

Choose one pupil each lesson to be your lead greeter. Their job is to welcome any visitor to the classroom and, using a copy of your lesson plan, be able to help the visitor see what progress you have made so far in the lesson – and how you have made it. This should prevent you having a forced mini-plenary if you want to stay in flow but give the inspector an insight into how well your pupils know what this lesson is about. Other roles for your classroom can be lead questioner,

Objective/learning outcomes	**Long-term personal goal**

By the end of this lesson you will be able to:

1. Note how the writer has used language effectively

2. Comment on how the writer uses language to engage the reader using quotations

I will read and understand great writing so that I can learn to write brilliantly myself

PLTs (teamworker): Show how well you work with others

I make a big difference to my team's performance through listening, working together and setting high standards

PLTs (independent enquirer): Work independently and find things out for myself

I can think about what I need to do to succeed in a task and do it really well on my own lead celebrator, literacy ambassador – all intended to give pupils responsibilities that challenge their comfort zone and support your classroom culture of high expectations for all.

Step 5. The main lesson activity/activities

This is where the teacher's expertise really counts to facilitate the learning and maximise progress. In outstanding classrooms pupils demonstrate that they can work really well together or on their own. Varying your activities will develop the flexibility that all learners need, and encourage good learning habits so that:

> 'Pupils love the challenge of learning and are resilient to failure. They are curious, interested learners who seek out and use new information to develop, consolidate and deepen their knowledge, understanding and skills. They thrive in lessons and also regularly take up opportunities to learn through extra-curricular activities.'
>
> Ofsted, *School inspection handbook* (2015): 49

In your classroom there needs to be:

1. A challenging level of subject knowledge – a passion for the subject and an ability to communicate it in ways that enthuse the students.

2. Active, collaborative learning – it is crucial to show students are able to work, on task, with and without adult supervision.

3. A choice of challenging activities or approaches available.

4. A competitive element, where appropriate.

5. Lots of higher order questions (which you don't answer for them). Every child should have the chance to ask and answer questions every lesson, whether in class, groups or pairs.

6. Visual aids and practical activities to apply the learning.

The first four points, **challenge**, **collaboration**, **choice** and **competition**, must be present to deliver an outstanding lesson because:

- **Challenge** is the way to ensure that expectations are high and learners are working to *make progress* in their learning.
- **Collaboration** ensures that *students* work together, independently of the teacher, to achieve brilliant outcomes.
- **Choice** engages the learners and makes them feel committed to the task.
- **Competition** encourages **commitment.** As John Hattie summarises, 'a major source of this commitment to school learning comes from peers – through pressure,

modelling and competition' (John Hattie, *Visible Learning for Teachers* (2012): 59) so it is the teacher's aim to encourage collaborative challenges that help students desire to be the very best learners in the classroom.

Most importantly, let the *students* lead the lesson. Give them the chance to talk more than the teacher and you will tap into the natural talents in the room. The teacher should not always be the 'sage on the stage' but an inspiring exposition can work well, particularly when it is embedded by applying the new knowledge in a practical activity. Use whatever teaching methods suit the material so long as they meet the learners' needs and help them fulfil their potential.

> 'Ofsted does not specify how planning should be set out, the length of time it should take or the amount of detail it should contain. Inspectors are interested in the effectiveness of planning rather than the form it takes.'
>
> Ofsted, *School inspection handbook* (2015): 11

Collaborative activities can help to connect the learning with the world at home and allow the teacher to be a facilitator of learning by intervening with individuals to challenge, support or scaffold tasks. This is the very best type of differentiation and in outstanding classroom teaching this will be evident and highly effective in meeting individual needs.

In addition, collaborative activities can be highly effective in inspiring pupils and ensuring that they learn extremely well. When you work with small groups they help you to hit many more of the 'outstanding' grade descriptors for quality of teaching by enabling you to:

- use your excellent subject knowledge to question, challenge and inspire pupils;
- check pupils' understanding in lessons and give support to those in need;
- give well-directed feedback which, in turn, the pupils respond to and make progress;
- foster effort and resilience to failure in your pupils and promote a love of learning and pride in their work;
- be able to report accurately on progress to parents and others.

> Managing great teamwork that helps learning progress is a key skill for an outstanding teacher.

You can also set up group work or teamwork that develops employability or personal skills (i.e. the PLTs). But before doing this, coach students in the four stages of group work: forming, storming, norming and performing (Tuckman 1965). Roles within groups and the skills needed for effective leadership also need to be taught.

Stand back and support students'
abilities to resolve conflict in group work.

Differentiation means setting different learning outcomes for different groups of students so they are all challenged to make good progress. When you set your outcomes make sure you describe the success criteria for different ability groups (even in streamed classes you will have a range of abilities).

Three useful beliefs which underpin outstanding teaching:

1. We always underestimate the capabilities of young people.

2. Every child wants to succeed.

3. We get what we expect.

Collaborative projects are group challenges that involve choosing tasks around a cross-curricular or single subject theme and completing them by negotiation. The end product will be demonstrated to the whole class and celebrated as part of the assessment.

Assessment for such projects can be subject based or skills based and this will depend on the learning outcomes that have been set and monitored by both teachers and students. There are two examples of collaborative projects below and more are available in *The Competency Curriculum Toolkit* by Jackie Beere and Helen Boyle. Note that these examples have both an element of choice in the tasks and an onus on completing the work as a team. The outcomes should be presented by the group and, as far as is possible, quality control should be given to the team.

An element of competition can be added by allocating points for different tasks; the following diagrams are a good example of this. The activities shown on page 28 are compulsory and an additional two activities should be chosen from page 29.

> Choice engages the emotional brain
> and enhances motivation for students.

Research Newton's First Law of Motion.
5 points

Research Newton's Third Law of Motion.
5 points

Research Newton's Second Law of Motion.
5 points

Build a water rocket.
10 points

Water Rocket Project

Compulsory activities.

Launch your rocket and measure the distance it travelled.
3 points

Write a detailed evaluation of the performance of your rocket.
5 points

What is PSI? Why is it important in launching a rocket?
5 points

Draw diagrams of your water rocket showing the forces acting on it at different times.
2 points

Present your project as a poem or rap.
2 points

Present a piece of drama work to illustrate Newton's Laws of Motion.
7 points

Water Rocket Project

Choose 2 other activities to complete.

Brainstorm for ideas on how to improve the performance of a water rocket.
2 points

Compare the performance of your rocket with that of another group.
2 points

Shoot a video of your rocket in flight.
2 points

Present your project as a news article.
5 points

Here is another example, this time points are not necessary.

Subject and skills links: English,
Food, History, ICT, Creative
Thinking, Teamworking.

Agree as a group the murder story for your party.

Create a menu for the meal.

Research at least 4 historical figures to invite to your party.

Murder Mystery Dinner Party

Design the invitations. Include a mystery riddle (optional).

Write the script for each guest to introduce themselves.

Design or describe the costumes for the guests.

Design your own tasks for the team.

See www.jackiebeere.com for more examples of collaborative projects.

Step 6. Dish up the DIRT ... often!

DIRT = Dedicated Improvement and Reflection Time through assessment *as* learning

The process of learning is a journey. It is essential to raise awareness of this by frequently reminding students to check their learning processes and progress. (What have you learned? How have you learned it? How far have you travelled towards the learning outcome?) There should be regular checkpoints in the lesson that become part of the assessment *as* learning process.

A very important part of this is the teacher's awareness of how different groups of students have performed and what their next steps should be (another good reason to do collaborative learning and not simply to lead from the front). Pay particular attention to the most and least able, special educational needs and disabilities (SEND) students, girls, boys, ethnic minorities, disadvantaged children and children in care etc. as appropriate. You need to know who these students are and how they have progressed. They need to know too!

In evaluating the accuracy and impact of assessment, inspectors will consider how well:

- teachers use any assessment for establishing pupils' starting points, teacher assessment and testing to modify teaching so that pupils achieve their potential by the end of a year or key stage; inspectors should note that Ofsted does not expect to see any particular system of assessment in place;

- assessment draws on a range of evidence of what pupils know, understand and can do across the curriculum;

- teachers make consistent judgements about pupils' progress and attainment, for example within a subject, across a year group and between year groups.

Ofsted, *School inspection handbook* (2015): 46

In addition, when inspectors are assessing *progress over time* they will scrutinise books and see if your pupils have responded to your feedback by addressing your constructive criticism. If the comment 'label your diagrams' is made it must be addressed by a pupil's response. A teacher reported recently having 'fix it' time in certain lessons when there is built-in time to read and respond to the formative feedback that has been given in marking. This fits in beautifully with your DIRT policy.

With DIRT you can help ensure that you hit these descriptors for the quality of teaching, learning and assessment:

> ■ Teachers provide adequate time for practice to embed the pupils' knowledge, understanding and skills securely. They introduce subject content progressively and constantly demand more of pupils. Teachers identify and support any pupil who is falling behind, and enable almost all to catch up.
>
> ■ Teachers check pupils' understanding systematically and effectively in lessons, offering clearly directed and timely support.
>
> ■ Teachers provide pupils with incisive feedback, in line with the school's assessment policy, about what pupils can do to improve their knowledge, understanding and skills. The pupils use this feedback effectively.
>
> ■ Pupils are eager to know how to improve their learning. They capitalise on opportunities to use feedback, written or oral, to improve.
>
> Ofsted, *School inspection handbook* (2015): 48–49

Your feedback must help your learners build resilience so that they can really deal effectively with constructive criticism and remain confident. DIRT sessions inoculate your learners against the fragile ego that can result from fake praise. They need to know exactly what they have done right and how to improve. As John Hattie stresses: 'Resilience is the ability to react to adversity, challenge, tension, or failure in an adaptive and productive manner' (John Hattie, *Visible Learning for Teachers* (2012): 59).

This resilience is a crucial habit to develop in our classrooms. Your DIRT session must remind learners who say 'I can't do this' that that sentence ends in … 'YET'.

Reviewing and reflecting

Ideally, students must be self-motivated, resilient and driven to make progress in their own learning.

This is the quality control moment when students work on their own or together to improve their work.

When students know what the success criteria are, then they are better able to gauge their progress. But they need to focus on the quality of the work produced too. A checklist that relates to success criteria is helpful here. You could enable students to begin to self- or peer-assess the work they produce to encourage independence.

Working to redraft, redraft again, improve and amend against success criteria and acting on constructive criticism is a vital part of the learning journey. It also gives the students more control over – and responsibility for – the outcomes. It also prevents marking from being a mysterious process that only goes on in the teacher's head.

> High quality self-assessment and peer-assessment gives learners the ability to discuss and develop their own progress.

WRITING	Emerging In most writing:
AF1 Write imaginative, interesting and thoughtful texts	▪ include relevant ideas ▪ try to add to basic information ▪ try to show a viewpoint even if I don't all the time
AF2 Produce texts which are appropriate to purpose, audience and style	▪ try to show the purpose ▪ try to use some features and the right style

WRITING	**Developing** **Across a range of writing:**
AF1 Write imaginative, interesting and thoughtful texts	■ choose relevant ideas ■ develop some ideas in detail and description while showing a clear viewpoint
AF2 Produce texts which are appropriate to purpose, audience and style	■ make the main purpose of my writing clear ■ use appropriate features ■ try to use the right style

WRITING	Mastering Across a range of writing:
AF1 Write imaginative, interesting and thoughtful texts	■ develop relevant ideas with some imagination ■ develop ideas suited to the form of writing ■ establish a consistent viewpoint
AF2 Produce texts which are appropriate to purpose, audience and style	■ maintain the purpose of my writing ■ show some features and the right style ■ adapt some features when I need to

Step 7. Final plenary/review

The moment of truth: how far did we get towards our objectives?

At the end of the lesson a memorable plenary will sum up the learning outcomes. *If students haven't all made progress don't be afraid to acknowledge it* and explain what your next steps will be to ensure they *all* have learned what they need to. Deep learning means reviewing and refreshing knowledge and applying it to new contexts. Test out their understanding by giving them problems to solve using what they have learned so far. For example, if you are teaching about how gases behave get them to blow up a balloon and put it in the freezer – then, next lesson, explain why it shrinks.

> Helping students to develop a language they can use to talk about their learning and how much progress they have made is an essential part of making assessment contribute to the process of learning.

Useful plenary techniques include:

- Having a huge learning progress arrow on the wall. Students pin their names on it to show how far they have progressed towards the learning outcome. They need to explain exactly what they have learned to progress to this place.

- Sticky notes for students to record three things they have learned – these can be placed on the door on the way out or shared in groups and prioritised.
- Mini-whiteboards and pens for writing down and showing key points from the lesson.
- Showing 5, 4, 3, 2, 1 fingers to indicate learning progress – 5 fingers means 'I really got it', 4 means 'I mostly got it', 3 means 'I got some of it' and so on.
- Students sit in a hotseat and make three points as a key character who would be an expert in the lesson outcome. They hand on to another class member who has to make two points, then down to one.
- Students write down the key learning points from the lesson on pieces of paper, fold them up and put them in a bag or box. Open it up next lesson and share the comments.
- Summarise the key learning in a headline. It is useful to have some mock-up newspapers made with blank headlines.

Always finish on time so that you don't miss out a final plenary that draws some conclusions about the learning. It provides vital information for planning your next lesson.

Know your impact! The final plenary

Cut short other activities if necessary, but make sure you have this chance to demonstrate the progress in learning and also make your own assessment about whether you have succeeded in achieving the learning outcome. You could also use the technique of briefing one of your students to be the lead greeter, who provides a summary of 'what we have learned so far' as he or she welcomes the visitor into the classroom (see page 20).

A neat way to assess the learning is to use 'exit tickets'. Hand out a ticket to everyone towards the end of the lesson. Each ticket has a few questions, graded in difficulty, which test understanding of the lesson objectives or how the knowledge might be applied to new contexts. If you have time, peer mark them before taking them in. Otherwise, collect them in as the pupils leave. No ticket, no exit! Before the next lesson analyse them for common mistakes or misconceptions so you know what they are and can prepare to address them. Start the next lesson with the answers to the ticket, or by taking some pupils aside as appropriate. The tickets could also include a space for them to comment on the lesson and what they thought of your teaching, for example, 'What would you like me to Keep, Grow or Change?'

It should be very clear to any observer that students have made progress in learning and can demonstrate it. Where insufficient progress has been made it should be clear what the plan of action will be to address this next lesson. One of the most common criticisms is that teachers don't use assessment outcomes to inform future planning. Make it clear that you can see what each and every student has learned and what the next steps are to secure progress.

Occasionally you could recap the learning by asking the pupils what they could put in their learning Rucksack, Treasure Chest or First-Aid Box. Get them to write down two or three learning points which they found useful to put in their Rucksack to help them in their future learning journey. If they have any 'learning treasure' – new skills which they can use again and again or light-bulb learning moments, they would go into the Treasure Chest for future use. Also ask if they have anything which they might put in the First-Aid Box – any problems or difficulties etc. Some teachers actually have a rucksack, a treasure chest and a first-aid box on the front desk for pupils to put their notes into.

Finish the plenary by setting the scene for the next exciting learning experience that will build on the lesson.

Our learners spend much of their time learning effectively at home – setting up their mobile phones, using social media and computer games. Make sure you link learning at school to learning at home – and cash in on their expertise!

Set homework or extended learning that connects with the progress made and links the learning to a wider context.

Top tip: Plenaries can take place throughout the lesson. Take a moment for a mini-plenary at any time in the session to gather evidence about the learning progress (especially if you have an observer or inspector with you). Moments taken to reflect on how the learning is progressing are an important part of an outstanding lesson.

Please note: There is no expected prescriptive structure to a lesson but you need to be clear about what you are teaching and how you will measure your impact. The best lessons are responsive to the pupils' needs so this requires flexibility.

Chapter 2

Preparing to be present in the classroom

I've learned that people will forget what you said, people will forget what you did, but people will never forget how you made them feel.

Maya Angelou

Preparing for the observer in your classroom: the mind–body connection

Your lesson is planned and you have your resources ready – including water to drink. Now start mentally rehearsing your lesson before you get there. This is an important part of your preparation. When you do the mental rehearsal, make sure that you are saying the phrases shown on pages 50 to 52. Also, see yourself with positive body language – standing up in control of the class but relaxed and smiling. Breathe deeply, slowly and regularly.

Imagine yourself doing the following during the lesson: meet and greet the students. Look as if you are enjoying it and hear your voice – strong, loud and authoritative, full of warmth and sincerity. Calm the class, praise, explain the objectives and tasks. Move around the classroom with confidence. Hover around the students who may need extra focus and give them positive attention when they are on task. Make sure you take a moment to breathe and assess how well the lesson is going. Always keep good eye contact on a one-to-one level.

> 'Teachers plan lessons very effectively, making maximum use of lesson time and coordinating lesson resources well. They manage pupils' behaviour highly effectively with clear rules that are consistently enforced.'
>
> Ofsted, *School inspection handbook* (2015): 48

Regularly sweep the room to ensure you know *everything* that is going on – both in front of you and behind your back. This is very important, especially when you have an official observer. Get into the habit of having eyes in the back of your head in every lesson. Nothing is more powerful than giving the message that you know exactly what is happening in one corner of the room even when you are helping students in the opposite corner. When students are working collaboratively and in teams your role is to move around and support their learning, but keep half of your attention on the whole classroom environment to ensure a positive working atmosphere.

So, the rehearsal is over and you are now prepared, confident and ready to be observed.

This is what I was born for ...

Being present in the classroom means that you are 'in the moment' and all your energy and focus is there. Our attention can easily be hijacked by visitors, distracting behaviour from certain individuals, activity outside the room, our own problems, nervousness about the situation and so on. Ruthlessly attend to the teaching you are delivering and allow nothing to divert you from this. We have all experienced that moment when you become conscious of the sound of your own voice speaking and this can lead to anxiety sabotaging our performance. Just stay in the moment, focus your conscious attention on what you are saying and on the students in your classroom. Don't allow your mind to wander. This way you will perform at your best and maintain the authenticity essential for the lesson to work well.

Practise what you preach

Great teachers have a philosophy that says, 'Every mistake is a learning experience.' Make sure that you endorse this philosophy in your own working life. You will have bad lessons – lessons that go horribly wrong and make you feel like you should give up. If you are unlucky, these experiences may happen when someone is observing. If you put into practice the philosophy of learning from your mistakes, and make this a habit of your teaching, then you will always be able to adapt when a lesson goes wrong. Firstly, admit your mistakes – especially to the students. Get feedback from them as to why it didn't work and learn from this. Secondly, recognise when it has gone wrong and try something different. Thirdly, appreciate you can't know everything – sometimes they will know more than you (especially about mobile phones!). Exploit this and get them to share their expertise. Be confident that being a teacher doesn't mean you have to know everything – but you do know your subject and how to help kids learn. One of the most impressive aspects of the best lessons is seeing students take over and do some of the teaching. Teaching each other is one of the best ways students can deepen learning. Do it often.

Finally, if the lesson takes an unexpected turn – but this new direction will serve to extend their learning – don't simply stick to your plan (even if the inspector has a copy of it). Explain that this is a great development and you are going to deviate a little to make the most of this new opportunity for learning. Make sure this isn't just a hobby horse of yours or of interest to only a small group of students. For example, one student may have a story that relates to the lesson; let them tell the story and then ask, 'What can we learn from this that fits with our learning outcome?'

Behaviour management

Working hard on building the consistent classroom relationships described above is the key to managing behaviour. Respect for each other and respect for the teacher should be habitual behaviours that characterise your teaching. If the lesson is interesting and expectations are high, behaviour management will not be a problem. Peer pressure can be a huge lever for learning; make it work for you by nurturing an atmosphere where *the students know that the more they support each other's learning, the more they will make outstanding progress themselves.* When students are speaking or answering, everyone in the classroom should want to help them make progress. There must be zero tolerance of mockery and put-downs and massive compliments for students who can offer constructive criticism and feedback which is given with love. This is what I mean by unconditional support; when it becomes a habit it takes place with or without the teacher in the classroom.

> 'Teachers are determined that pupils achieve well. They encourage pupils to try hard, recognise their efforts and ensure that pupils take pride in all aspects of their work. Teachers have consistently high expectations of all pupils' attitudes to learning.'
>
> Ofsted, *School inspection handbook* (2015): 49

With the above in place, students will then want to support you and do well themselves on the day of the inspection. Enlist their support and be open about what will happen when an observer speaks to them and asks them about their learning. Encourage them to be open and honest and answer in as much detail as possible. Be clear about how important they are to this process of judging the lesson and the school. Often teachers say, 'This is not about you being inspected, it's about me. So don't worry.' This is just not true – and they know it. Their books will be checked and they will be asked questions and listened to. How they respond will be an important part of the judgement so explain why all this happens and describe how they can talk about their learning and progress.

If any students behave badly, address the behaviour and follow through with any sanctions. Follow the school's behaviour policy (not your own version) rigorously and consistently in all your lessons and do the same when you are observed. If an observer or inspector sees you deal firmly and effectively with any incident you will create a very positive impression.

Make sure you have specific strategies to deal with those more challenging individuals in your class to ensure that, in your lesson, they want to learn and they know for sure you deal with them consistently, rigorously and *never* give up on them.

Love your students

It is a basic tenet of neuroscience that learning is an emotional experience. Nothing is more important than you and the aura that you project in the classroom. This includes your relationship with the students and your belief in yourself as a great teacher. As Independent Thinking Associate Dr Andrew Curran says in the introduction to his *The Little Book of Big Stuff about the Brain*: 'The most surprising message for me from looking through billions of dollars of research is that the most important thing you can do for yourself and for others is to love yourself and others for who they are, because by doing that you maximise the brain's ability to learn and unlearn.'

Loving your students can require high quality acting and performing skills! But, as many teachers have discovered, such performances can become a reality. You can learn to love them – even the 'hardcore' students; the ones who seem determined to make you dislike them by challenging your authority and who refuse to participate in learning activities that have taken hours of careful thought and planning. Many of us have surprised ourselves using that tried and tested method of 'pretending' that your least favourite class is, in fact, the class you most enjoy teaching. How do you do this? Simple! Arrive early, instead of as late as possible. Wait with a smile at the door and a personal greeting, especially for the most challenging individuals. Set the highest expectations of behaviour and learning in your opening communications and be consistent in sticking to them in every lesson and with every student.

Great communication and rapport

Communication skills are the most crucial skills that a teacher needs to ensure the best outcomes in lessons – but it is so easy to get it wrong. Rapport exists when you have a connection with your audience which makes their emotional brain feel good and want to be there. You know when you have it when people listen, smile and respond to you.

When you don't have it, you can be as knowledgeable and clever as you like, but no one will be listening.

You get rapport through using an appropriate register. Make it too formal and the students will turn off. Use open, confident body language, good volume and intonation that sounds enthusiastic – even passionate – about your subject. Adapt and tune in to the mood of the classroom. Connect with their world by understanding it. Music, sport, television, computer games, gangs – whatever it takes – make sure you know what will connect with them and try to use it in your teaching. Your job is to create a 'can do' and 'will do' philosophy and to nurture an atmosphere where making mistakes is accepted as an integral part of learning. Be consistent in this. *Every* lesson!

It is the habits of your learners that you are developing each and every day that will make your lesson and your school 'outstanding'.

Here are some simple examples of good and poor verbal communication.

Good verbal communication: what to say

'Good morning! How is my favourite class today?'

'Anything exciting happen at the weekend?'

'I'm really looking forward to teaching you this bit as you're going to love it.'

'I was really impressed with what some of you did for homework. It's some of the best work I've ever seen.'

'Some of you have found it hard but that's good because we are going to learn why, sort it out and get you making great progress.'

'We'll find a way to help you learn this.'

'You are the best class I teach.'

'I love the way you work together so well.'

'You've come up with the most amazing ideas.'

'You've made my day with the work you've produced.'

'I need you to listen and work hard because I know you can do it.'

'When you're at football practice you're so determined. Let's see if you can find some of that motivation and apply it here for me.'

'The way this class supports each other in their learning is outstanding and makes me very proud.'

'No matter what happens I will never give up on you because I know you can be a great learner.'

'Well done for working so hard on that. Tell me what you've learned so far and what else you would like to learn.'

'Brilliant. That work you are doing shows just how hard you're working. What do you need to do to progress further?'

'You're thinking really hard about what you have to do and you'll really make great progress like this.'

'You've redrafted this so many times and that's exactly what you need to do to produce an outstanding piece of writing. Superb effort!'

'You didn't get that right but you kept trying and learned from your mistakes – that makes you a brilliant learner.'

> 'Parents think that they can hand children permanent confidence – like a gift – by praising their brains and talent. It doesn't work, and in fact has the opposite effect. It makes children doubt themselves as soon as anything is hard or anything goes wrong. If parents want to give their children a gift, the best thing they can do is teach their children to love challenges, be intrigued by mistakes, enjoy effort, and keep on learning.'
>
> Carol Dweck, *Mindset* (2006): 176–177

Dweck's research work shows us that in order to develop a 'growth mindset' it is not enough to tell students just to work harder or get an A grade. You need to help them develop strategies for learning and thinking that work for their individual needs and praise their efforts in doing this more than praising the outcome.

Praise them when they are making progress through persistence and determination. Never give false praise.

Poor verbal communication: what not to say

'Let's not have another lesson where we waste your time and mine.'

'We have to get through this bit for the exam even though it's hard and boring.'

'I can't believe how many of you just haven't made the effort for homework. You'll never learn anything unless you make more effort.'

'You're really struggling with this so you need to concentrate harder.'

'You're the worst class in Year 8 because you just don't listen.'

'If you don't get on with your work you're wasting my time, so I'll waste your time in break.'

'I don't enjoy this any more than you do.'

'I am so disappointed in the way you are behaving.'

'What would your parents say if they saw the way you are behaving.'

Praising the outcome alone can make students think that only this is important and that the effort, skills and strategies they used are less so. Also, some students who get praised for excellent results may become reluctant to try harder challenges if they think that they won't succeed and so learn to limit their learning. So don't say:

'Brilliant, 10/10 – a fantastic result. Keep this up.'

'This is A grade work – well done.'

'At last, a C grade – keep this up!'

'Getting there.'

'That's brilliant!' (When it plainly isn't.)

Chapter 3
Assessment *as* learning

AfL [assessment for learning] is the process of seeking and interpreting evidence for use by students and their teachers, to decide where the students are in their learning, where they need to go and how best to get there.

Rowe (2007)

Assessment is such an important part of the process of learning, and of making progress in learning, that it deserves a chapter in its own right. The argument put by Dylan Wiliam and Paul Black in *Inside the Black Box* has been won and assessment for learning policy and practice has been driving school improvement strategies because it works. (For more information visit http://weaeducation.typepad.co.uk/files/blackbox-1.pdf.)

Assessment *as* learning takes the effective practice of AfL a step further as it recognises that assessment is itself an integral part of the learning process.

An observer will expect your students to be able to talk about their learning and what they need to do to improve. They will expect to see evidence in the work they have produced of focused marking and targets for improvement, with clear evidence of pupils responding to feedback and making progress over time. Make sure there is evidence of this in the students' books or notes.

An assessment-centred classroom has been described as follows:

'In assessment-centred classrooms, assessment is both formative and summative and becomes a tool to aid learning: students monitor their progress over time and with their teachers identify the next steps needed to improve. Techniques such as open questioning, sharing learning objectives and focused marking have a powerful effect on students' ability to take an active role in their learning. There is always sufficient time left for reflection by students. Whether individually or in pairs, students are given the opportunity to review what they have learned and how they have learned it. They evaluate themselves and one another in a way that contributes to understanding. Students know their levels of achievement and make progress towards their next goal.'

Hargreaves (2005)

This type of teaching clearly encourages independent learning as it gives students the tools for monitoring their own progress. It also links clearly to the Personal, Learning and Thinking skills (PLTs) as it involves the development of reflective learning, self-management and independent enquiry.

Now compare your own practice against the following top tips for 'perfect' assessment *as* learning.

The lesson objectives/learning outcomes?

What are you trying to achieve this lesson? This is the only question that matters. Your objective can be a question you are trying to answer, a skill to develop or some knowledge you are trying to help them acquire.

The objective doesn't have to be at the beginning, it doesn't have to be written in books but it should be understood by all ... exactly what is it we are trying to learn today? *All* your pupils must engage with *what* they are learning and *why* they are doing it. They also need to see the point of the objectives in the bigger picture; that is, how they relate to the last lesson's learning, the course they are following and the big overall goal. This means that you can't simply write the objectives on the board and hope that the students merely copy them down. In fact copying them down could waste valuable learning time. The students should engage with your objectives and be able to explain them to the observer.

1. All the learners should be able to see where they are and what they need to do to make more progress. This should link into subject standards and progression where possible. It is crucial to have high expectations of what can be achieved and engage the students with that belief.

2. Success criteria for achieving the outcomes need to be negotiated with the students for optimum engagement and to enable them to be clear about what it will look like and feel like and sound like when they have made that progress.

Consider the example below of a learning outcome and differentiated success criteria for an English functional skills lesson. It includes differentiated learning outcomes and shows a visual image of how this represents progress towards a bigger goal which relates to life and other subjects. Students can also mark along this arrow where they think they are at the end of the lesson to show progress (or – just as important – lack of it). Be careful that differentiated objectives don't cap the effort of, or outcome for, some students. (This can happen with the 'some, most, all' type models.) Everyone should be aiming for the highest outcome and finding a way to get there over time.

OBJECTIVE: To recognise the power of different types of language *or* How is language powerful in different ways?

OUTCOMES: I will be able to:

- Use formal and informal language.
- Explain how to speak and write in appropriate language.
- Teach others how to use a range of writing and speaking styles appropriate for different audiences.

Where am I now on the path to the big goal?

| Entry level | | | | Level 1 | | | | Level 2 |

I will be able to use language to be a successful communicator at work and in life.

Self-assessment

You need to encourage the habit of self-assessment against the learning objectives until it becomes routine. The assessment objectives for your subject may help with this but they will probably need translating into simple categories as in the table below showing the levels, or if you would prefer, graded descriptors, for the assessment of reading.

> I have come to the conclusion that my mood and my motivation are a mirror to reflect the mood and motivation of my class.

Level 1	Level 2
✓ I can read aloud words I read a lot. ✓ I can understand what more difficult words mean because I know the alphabet, but I sometimes need help. ✓ I can say why I like some poems and stories.	✓ I can read and understand easy pieces of writing. ✓ I can often work out how to say a word and what it means if I do not know it. ✓ I can say what I think about things which have happened in the story, poem or other writing.

Level 3	Level 4
✓ I can read aloud clearly and without making many mistakes. ✓ I can usually work out what a word means by myself. ✓ I can understand what happens in what I read and can explain what I like and what I do not like. ✓ I can find books in the library, use a dictionary and an index because I know the alphabet.	✓ When I read a story I can say who is in it (the characters) and what happens (the events). ✓ When I read a piece of writing, I can say what it is about (the themes). ✓ I can try to guess what happens in a story and make guesses about why characters do things. ✓ When I talk or write about something I've read I can show someone what I mean in the book. I can find out what I want to know from books.

Level 5	Level 6
✓ I can say what is important about what I have read. ✓ I use examples and quotations from what I have read to show what I mean. ✓ I can find out what I want to know from books and other sources of information.	✓ I can see that there may be more than one meaning to texts I have read and I can explain why these are important. ✓ I can say what I think about books, poems and plays by looking at the way they are written (the language and the structure) and the themes. ✓ I can research something I want to know from lots of different sources and write it down.

Level 7	Level 8
✓ I can say how writers use language to say what they want to say. ✓ I can write about themes, structure and the way language is used (linguistic features) in poems, plays and novels. ✓ I can select information from many sources and use it in different ways.	✓ I can write about how an author uses linguistic features, structure and the layout of the text (presentational devices) to influence the reader. ✓ I can select what is relevant in a text and look at how the same information can be presented differently in different types of texts.

Exceptional performance

✓ I can write in detail, develop my ideas and look carefully at the language, structure and presentation of a range of demanding texts.

✓ I can make comparisons between texts including audience, purpose and form.

✓ I can see when information is presented as argument or opinion.

Note: With thanks to TES Resources.

Peer-assessment

Opportunities for peer-assessment are vital in a great lesson. When an observer sees this happening really well in your classroom it will be because you have built up the skills to do it well over time. This, in turn, provides excellent evidence of the quality of your teaching. To nurture great peer-assessment you need to show students how important they are to each other's learning. Use the following five point plan:

1. Teach students that 'I can learn more by helping others learn', and that when they assess each other's work it improves their own performance. After all, having played the role of assessor they know what is required to impress.

2. Create a culture of unconditional support of each other's learning. Reinforce an atmosphere where the students

listen to each other, care about each other making good progress and appreciate constructive criticism.

3. Have zero tolerance of disrespect for the effort of others. This must apply when students are marking each other's work or when they are listening to each other's presentations.

4. Make sure they know and understand the success criteria when assessing each other's work. They can then write targets for each other as they mark each other's work. This will help them to understand how to improve their own work too.

5. Reward high quality peer-assessment as much as you can.

Teacher questioning

More effort has to be spent in framing questions that are worth asking: that is, questions that explore issues that are critical to the development of children's understanding.

Black et al. (2003)

Use open questions that encourage analysis, synthesis and evaluation at critical learning moments to elicit thinking and develop learning. You can do this when students are working on an individual basis or in class discussion.

Work at the top end of Bloom's taxonomy

In the classroom teachers usually concentrate on teaching the lower-order skills in Bloom's taxonomy. However, we need students to use higher-order skills to make learning last. Examples of verbs and question stems, and some activities for each level, are given in the tables on pages 66 to 68.

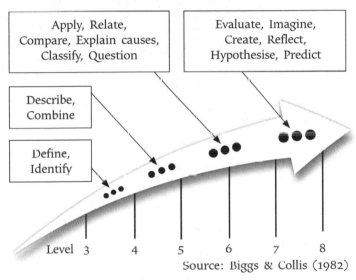

Source: Biggs & Collis (1982)

Many teachers have found the use of the above SOLO taxonomy to be even more useful for differentiating cognitive processes and planning activities to challenge thinking. See www.jackiebeere.com for examples of activities.

Increasing demand: The following tables further illustrate the top three skills.

Creating

Skill/activity	Verbs	Question stems
Creating Invent a machine to ... Design a ... Write a ... about ...	Imagine. Generalise. Relate. Predict. Conclude. Combine. Modify. Re-arrange. Substitute. Plan. Design. Create. Invent. Compose. Formulate. Prepare. Generalise. Re-write.	Can you design a ... to ... ? Why not compose a song about ... ? Can you see a possible solution to ... ? What would happen if ... ? How many ways can you ... ? Can you create new uses for ... ? Can you make a new recipe for ... ? Can you develop a proposal to ... ?

Increasing demand ←

Evaluating

Skill/activity	Verbs	Question stems
Evaluating Prepare a case to present your view about ... Convince others that ...	Test. Measure. Rank/grade. Discriminate between. Assess. Verify. Judge. Decide. Select. Choose. Recommend. Convince. Support. Summarise.	Is there a better solution to ... ? Judge the value of ... Can you defend your position about ... ? Is ... a good or a bad thing? How would you have handled ... ? What would you recommend and why? How effective are ... ? What do you think about ... ?

Increasing demand

67

Analysing

Skill/activity	Verbs	Question stems
Analysing Design a questionnaire to … Conduct an investigation to … Construct a graph to show …	Analyse. Identify. Recognise. See patterns. Select. Order. Organise. Classify. Arrange. Separate. Divide. Explain. Connect. Compare. Contrast. Infer.	How was this similar to … ? What was the underlying theme of … ? What are other possible outcomes? Can you explain what happened when … ? Can you distinguish between … ? What were the motives behind … ? What was the problem with … ?

Source: Bloom (1956)

Increasing demand ◄

These strategies are helpful when implementing successful questioning in the classroom.

Have a no hands-up policy

If no one can put their hand up, they all have to think about the question – especially when you then pick a name from a hat and expect an answer.

Thinking time: pair and share

Set questions they can think about in pairs and get them to come up with several possible answers to share with the rest of the class.

Use connectives to extend thinking

Ask them to use connectives such as 'but', 'therefore', 'however' or 'alternatively' like batons to extend answers. When a student answers, the next one must take over the answer and continue after the connective.

Reflect and review

Use metacognition to reflect on *what* has been learned and *how* it has been learned. As well as identifying what supported the learning, reflect on the mistakes made and the obstacles that got in the way (resources, research, friends, trying a different method, etc.).

Ask the students to make up a set of questions about what they have learned and what questions they need to ask for the next stage of their progress. This will require demonstrating an understanding of what they have learned and where they are now.

Pose, pause, pounce, bounce

This idea, based on Dylan Wiliam's work, is that questions should be posed by the teacher or other students, followed by a pause to allow everyone to think or discuss possible answers. One student is then pounced on for their answer and then their answer is bounced to a different student with another question like 'Do you agree with that answer?' and then to another student 'How can we find out if that is right?' The aim is to involve as many students as possible in the thinking process.

Try answering all questions with a question for an interesting lesson.

Assessment for learning in the classroom: what is an observer looking for?

Good
(the students do all of this):

- All students know what they are learning and why.
- Students know the success criteria and can self-assess their work against them.

- Students learn openly from each other frequently.
- Students ask reflective questions of their own and other's work.
- Students can constructively criticise each other to support learning.
- All students make good progress with developing independence.

Outstanding
(the students do all of the above *plus* all of this):

- All students understand and can talk about their learning outcomes and set their own individual success criteria.
- Students can use subject terminology as well as a language for learning to discuss and monitor their own progress.
- Students value talking for learning and consciously use it to advance their learning.
- Student questions demonstrate fearless enquiry and a desire to progress.
- Students know exactly where they are, what they have achieved and how to make further progress.

Good
(*you* do all of this):

- Plan and set challenging, differentiated and clear objectives.
- Students are encouraged to set success criteria for the learning outcomes.

- Links are made to other subjects and contexts.
- Grades of progression are known.
- Progress is reviewed with students regularly throughout the lesson.
- The teacher uses skilful questioning and resources to encourage sustained successful collaborative work.
- The teaching is flexible and responds to learning needs – adjusting whenever appropriate to make maximum progress.
- Marking is focused and sets clear targets that relate to learning needs and engages students so they take action.

Outstanding
(you do all of the above *plus* all of this):

- The teacher sets big goals and has very high expectations of all students in the lesson and over time.
- Progression in the Personal, Learning and Thinking skills and subject concepts is integral to the planning of the lesson.
- The teacher is constantly coaching students in understanding how their learning is progressing and how to recognise it.
- Class discussion is skilfully developed to nurture thinking and encourage independence.
- The teacher and the students develop the learning together in response to the advancement made.
- The teacher plans next steps with students in response to the progress made in the lesson.

■ There is clear evidence that marking impacts on students by helping them to make exceptional progress.

AfL in your heart and mind

The most important and powerful aspect of assessment *as* learning is that it is not a tick list of activities but it is *your* clear engagement with the process of learning, coaching your pupils to move relentlessly forward in their knowledge, skills and understanding. This will be an integral and flexible part of your teaching evident to any inspector when they listen to you, talk to the pupils, look in their books and see their progress over time. It is very clear in the latest guidance that a key part of the process of evaluating teaching in your school will be based around how effective assessment is in supporting progress.

Inspectors will consider: [...] scrutiny of pupils' work, with particular attention to:

■ pupils' effort and success in completing their work, both in and outside lessons, so that they can progress and enjoy learning across the curriculum

■ the level of challenge and whether pupils have to grapple appropriately with content, not necessarily 'getting it right' first time, which could be evidence that the work is too easy

■ how well teachers' feedback, written and oral, is used by pupils to improve their knowledge, understanding and skills

Ofsted, *School inspection handbook* (2015): 46

It is worth noting here that Ofsted does not expect to see a particular frequency or quantity of work in pupils' folders.

> Ofsted recognises that marking and feedback to pupils, both written and oral, are important aspects of assessment. However, Ofsted does not expect to see any specific frequency, type or volume of marking and feedback; these are for the school to decide through its assessment policy. Marking and feedback should be consistent with that policy, which may cater for different subjects and different age groups of pupils in different ways, in order to be effective and efficient in promoting learning.
>
> While inspectors will consider how written and oral feedback is used to promote learning, Ofsted does not expect to see any written record of oral feedback provided to pupils by teachers.
>
> Ofsted, *School inspection handbook* (2015): 11

Chapter 4
Independent learning in the classroom

Who works hardest in your classroom — you or the students? In your lessons are your students willing to ask questions, take decisions, select appropriate resources independently and learn from mistakes – or are they dependent on you?

To develop the habits of independent learning amongst your students takes time and skill, and consistency of approach across the school, but is rewarded in the long run. You will be less exhausted, your students will be more empowered and successful – and the teaching and learning across the school is more likely to be graded outstanding! There is no guaranteed formula for balance between your expert delivery and follow up group work. Neither will inspectors expect you to follow a prescribed planning or lesson format. The spotlight is on the learners. The more chance they have to demonstrate their ability to self-manage and work collaboratively, the more powerful their commitment to learning will appear.

'Pupils are confident, self-assured learners. Their excellent attitudes to learning have a strong, positive impact on their progress. They are proud of their achievements and of their school.'

Ofsted, *School inspection handbook* (2015): 52

'Pupils are typically able to articulate their knowledge and understanding clearly in an age-appropriate way. They can hold thoughtful conversations about them with each other and adults.'

Ofsted, *School inspection handbook* (2015): 57

Outstanding learning requires that you demonstrate in lessons that students are fully and personally engaged in the work that they are doing. Students should not be driven by the teacher directing the activities or controlling the outcomes. Nor should they be reliant on the teacher to provide the motivation through carrot or stick. Ideally, students must be self-motivated, resilient and driven to make progress in their own learning.

How do we achieve this if all classrooms are built on the didactic principle that the teacher knows best and knows all? Expert, passionate teachers are essential for great learning and the role of direct delivery clearly has a place. However, at times it can seem that in these classrooms the teacher has control of the key that unlocks the secret knowledge required for exam success. And teachers do have this key: the expertise built from years of accumulated knowledge and the experience of techniques that work to enable their students to pass exams. Teachers enjoy the power that this gives them when students want to learn. There is no better feeling than having a class hanging on to your every word as you 'stage the reveal' in a poem or scientific theory or show the quick way to remember a formula in maths.

However, the role of the teacher when it comes to developing independence in the learner is that of a knowledgeable, highly skilled mentor who is passionate about giving students the skills to find out *for themselves*. This is disparaged by some as child-centred, time-wasting nonsense that distracts from the important job of transferring information from the wise, learned head of the teacher into the empty, eager young mind of the student, through listening and copying from books and the board; a process whose validity is then supported by success in the narrow confines of a written test or exam.

However, the neuroscience of learning shows that this type of learning is superficial and quickly evaporates. Finding out information for themselves and then presenting, performing and teaching it to each other is a far more powerful way of creating learning that lasts. This type of learning is even more important for helping retain information and concepts and so for passing end of course examinations which have little or no coursework element.

'Finding new ways to nurture independent and creative thinkers is a key part of preparing children for life, work and play in today's changing society.'

Steve Beswick, Director of Education, Microsoft UK

John Crossland worked with advanced skills teachers (ASTs) to discover how brain-based research could be used to help improve learning in the classroom. He found that the ASTs were 'convinced that their already outstanding practice had significantly improved' through using Cognitive Acceleration through Science Education (CASE) thinking skills packages, which encourage collaborative, reflective learning based around the underlying principle that all learning has an emotional component.

However, even these excellent teachers still found it hard to let go of the control that the didactic model of teaching promotes: 'They often struggled to implement the counter-intuitive technique of standing back from intervening (non-intervention) in the learning processes during pupil collaborative group work and encouraging pupil metacognition (thinking about thinking) during the review/plenary' (Crossland 2010).

Teachers don't like to feel superfluous to requirements and often have such a strong work ethic that they feel a compulsion to be in control and want to be needed for their expert input. This is why even ASTs needed help to let go of the didactic model and encourage more independent learning habits in their students. However, many teachers (particularly those teaching vocational subjects) are already very good at this facilitation model of pedagogy. Some individuals find it a challenge not to be the 'sage on the stage' as opposed to 'the guide from the side', but most teachers can expand their professional ability in this area and enjoy the rewards of seeing students 'turning their own light bulbs on' by developing for themselves the required learning skills.

Leadership roles in the classroom

Giving roles on badges/lanyards such as:

- Lead questioner – the pupil who will ask an excellent question.
- Literacy/Numeracy ambassador – the pupil who can look out for language or number learning opportunities or mistakes.
- Lead celebrator – the pupil who can highlight something excellent happening in their class or group.
- Lead greeter – the pupil who greets an observer and briefs them about the lesson objective, process and progress of learning so far.
- Learning spy – the pupil in each group who scans other groups for great ideas to bring back and develop.
- Resilience guru – the pupil who can demonstrate how they overcame challenges.

These roles and any others you (or the pupils) can think of will enhance challenge, differentiation and motivation in the classroom. (More examples can be found at www.jackiebeere. com/resources.)

How to develop independent learning in the classroom

To start, raise awareness of and then teach the learning skills, using the Personal, Learning and Thinking skills (PLTs) as a framework. Students can be taught to focus on exactly what the skills of an 'independent enquirer' are and on how well they are applying them.

The PLTs have evolved from the 'learning to learn' theory and are identified as the skills required by employers:

Independent enquirers
Young people who process and evaluate information in their investigations, planning what to do and how to go about it. They take informed and well-reasoned decisions, recognising that others have different beliefs and attitudes.

Creative thinkers
Young people who think creatively by generating and exploring ideas and making original connections. They try different ways to tackle a problem, working with others to find imaginative solutions and outcomes that are of value.

Reflective learners

Young people who evaluate their strengths and limitations as learners and set themselves realistic goals and criteria for success. They monitor their own performance and progress, inviting feedback from others and making changes to improve their learning.

Teamworkers

Young people who work confidently with others, adapting to different contexts and taking responsibility for their own role. They listen and take account of other's views. They form collaborative relationships, resolving issues to reach agreed outcomes.

Self-managers

Young people who organise themselves, showing personal responsibility, initiative, creativity and enterprise with a commitment to learning and self-improvement. They actively embrace change, responding positively to new priorities, coping with challenges and looking for opportunities.

Effective participators

Young people who actively engage with issues that affect them and those around them. They play a full part in the life of their school, college, workplace or wider community by taking responsible action to bring improvements for others as well as themselves.

All of the above skills and dispositions prepare your students for future destinations and help address the 2015 Ofsted focus on spiritual, moral, social and cultural (SMSC) development when students show:

- a sense of enjoyment and fascination in learning about themselves, others and the world around them;
- use of imagination and creativity in their learning;
- willingness to reflect on their experiences;
- understanding of the consequences of their behaviour and actions;
- interest in investigating and offering reasoned views about moral and ethical issues and ability to understand and appreciate the viewpoints of others on these issues;
- willingness to participate in a variety of communities and social settings, including by volunteering, cooperating well with others and being able to resolve conflicts effectively.

It is important to develop all of the PLTs in the classroom – but good, independent learners need first to become good, independent enquirers. Good independent enquirers have the following skills. They:

- Identify clearly the questions to answer and problems to sort out.
- Plan and carry out research and understand how choices affect outcome.

■ Explore issues and events or problems from different points of view.

■ Analyse information and judge how important it is.

■ Understand how decisions and events can be affected by the situation, people's beliefs and feelings.

■ Back up their conclusions using thoughtful arguments and reasoning.

The following table gives a good starting point for students to consider how well-developed their independent enquiry skills are.

Logging the development of independent enquiry skills	Activities to develop the skills	Links to other PLTs/subjects
I identify questions to answer and problems to sort out Never Sometimes Usually Always ↑	Survival challenge on a desert island Plan a holiday Organise a charity fundraising event Five whys	*Teamworker* Science RS Citizenship PSHE
I plan and carry out research and understand how choices affect outcome Never Sometimes Usually Always ↑	Use search engines to research a topic in groups. Use different key words then compare the results Undertake a survey to assess student attitudes using different questions Compare the impact of questions on results	*Reflective learner* ICT English

Logging the development of independent enquiry skills	Activities to develop the skills	Links to other PLTs/subjects
I explore issues and events or problems from different points of view Never Sometimes Usually Always →	Take a current national, local or school subject issue: ■ PMI (Plus, Minus, Interesting) bits ■ Six Thinking Hats ■ Eight Way Thinking Tool ■ Role play edition of *Question Time* or *The Jeremy Kyle Show*	*Effective partici-pator* Citizenship RS
I analyse information and judge how important it is Never Sometimes Usually Always →	Examine several sources and place them in order of importance (e.g. newspaper article, encyclopaedia entry, horoscope, government White Paper statements, novel extract, graph, road sign)	*Reflective learner* Science History English

Logging the development of independent enquiry skills	Activities to develop the skills	Links to other PLTs/subjects
I understand how decisions and events can be affected by the situation, people's beliefs and feelings Never Sometimes Usually Always	Collect images and film clips with an emotive quality In groups discuss what is happening, why and what will happen next Evaluate and feedback how these answers were reached	*Creative thinker* Media/Art English
I back up my conclusions using thoughtful arguments and reasons Never Sometimes Usually Always	Use connectives to draw out detailed responses. Hold up a card with one of these on whenever a student thinks they have finished summing up a conclusion (e.g. but, also, because, however, alternatively, nevertheless, although, unless, except, for example, whereas, or)	*Self-manager* English History

Once students have become aware of the skills required for independent learning – and of the need to continually develop them and how they link to all subjects – then the scene is set to enable the students to demonstrate the independent learning skills they will need to thrive in the uncertain world beyond education. The long-term outcome will be to develop in our students the deep, sustainable learning habits that will also, believe it or not, ensure success in exams.

> 'Students need the attitudes and skills of independence for long term success ... Ironically, independence that is built into many primary schools during Key Stages 1 and 2 is dismantled in many secondary schools during Key Stage 3, only to be required again at Key Stage 4 [and even more so at Key Stage 5!].'
>
> Ginnis (2002)

Seven steps to independent learning

1. **Set big long-term goals** which will influence the learning outcomes of each lesson. We always underestimate what our students can do and a crucial measure of your success will be *how high your expectations are*. Give the students the bigger picture of how their lives can be altered for the better. Go beyond the classroom, school and exams towards life and personal success in order to engage the emotional brain.

2. **Have clear, required learning outcomes and skills to be developed** planned into individual lessons. Around 70 per cent of the lesson must be *collaborative work and active learning*. This means students talking with each other and doing. Build in maximum *choice* of activity to facilitate self-differentiation. Allow *flexibility* as the nature of these lessons means that the students may work faster or differently to expectation, and your job is to adjust the framework for maximum progress. Build in a *surprise* such as an additional resource or change of brief to encourage resilience. Plan *reflective strategies* that encourage self-assessment of the learning at several stages and at the end of the lesson.

3. **Set the emotional environment for learning** by delivering your input with passion and enthusiasm. It has to matter to you in order to engage the emotional brains of your students. Ensure that the groups are skilled in understanding how important good teamwork is through preparation and coaching in team roles and dynamics. Especially important is a feeling of safety and support amongst the group for the whole team. This can be enhanced over time by rewarding good leadership and inclusive behaviours.

4. **Include challenge and competition** to enhance the team-building process. Setting teams to compete against each other for points or throwing in additional unexpected challenges all help to unite them and focus their activity.

5. **Plan your interventions into their group work.**
   Allow the students themselves, as far as possible, to
   work through the problems they may have with the
   task and with group relationships. If you do need to
   intervene or help, limit the number of questions they
   can ask you by issuing question cards. Ensure that these
   questions promote metacognition (thinking about
   thinking). Encourage the students to find out answers
   for themselves. Always answer a question with a
   question. Discuss a solution with one team member and
   get him or her to teach it to the rest of the group.

6. **Use assessment as learning.** When students complete
   the tasks assigned they should each:

   ▨ critically appraise the work they have completed;
   ▨ discuss their role in the outcome;
   ▨ say how well they have met the objectives;
   ▨ crucially, say what *progress* they have made.

   The notes the students make will inform the quality
   control aspect of the learning outcome. A simple way
   for students to remember this is that they will need
   AIMS (Amend, Improve, Measure and Share
   (peer-assess)). They will need to do this several times
   during a project before they can become proficient at
   assessing and demonstrating their learning.

7. **Review and reflection.** When students have been
   working outside your supervision in a lesson this is

your chance to monitor how much they have achieved. They can log their skills in independent learning using the first column in the tables above (pages 84–86. How much of this did they do and can they tell you when and where? Can they demonstrate the skill they have acquired or the learning progress they have made? Can they say to each other, on a sticky note or in class discussion, *how* they learned it, motivated themselves, solved problems, worked with others and so on?

This important reflection is in addition to the mini-plenaries or assessment for learning strategies. It is a planned period of metacognition about the whole activity or project that links learning to home, big goals and other subjects. This could entail keeping a learning log or making a presentation to the class about how the learning worked and how their skills in independent learning are developing. Such a performance will enhance their recognition of progress and develop their language for learning. This reflective practice will help them learn from their mistakes and have a critical appreciation of their work, as well as an understanding of what motivates them.

It can take a lifetime to understand how to make the best of our own amazing learning preferences and potential – most of that lifetime journey takes place once we have left school. Why does work teach us so much more about the best way to learn?

Chapter 4

Embedding learning skills for life

By using the previous strategies consistently across the curriculum and over time, the students will develop their interpersonal skills, confidence, self-reliance, risk taking and the ability to challenge their own and other's thinking. These are skills which students use without thinking when mastering a new mobile phone, computer game, downloading music, using Facebook or learning a new dance.

The teacher's role is to highlight the *process* of learning in their classrooms and develop a language which describes that process. Teachers must also give students opportunities to own the process for themselves and to reflect on their learning. Independent learning in the classroom, in essence, simply taps into, further reinforces and makes explicit the pre-existing skills and motivation within our students. If we can provide the right stimuli and encourage their commitment to succeed, we will ensure that our students develop real, deep, lasting learning and a set of life skills which will more effectively equip them for the real world. And, oh yes, exam grades will improve too!

'Success in exams is still considered important but is increasingly viewed as the secondary result of excellent learning.'

2010 presentation by Ofsted Inspector Rob Hubbleday
('citing Ofsted 2009')

Chapter 5

Making teamwork work: productive collaborative learning

This chapter focuses on how to ensure that the collaborative work you do with students when being observed is hooked quite firmly into the *progress* in learning that we want to achieve. For many fabulous examples and ideas for group work activity see *The Teacher's Toolkit* by Paul Ginnis.

Use the Personal, Learning and Thinking skills (PLTs) model to ensure that students become aware of the importance of the *explicit* development of thinking skills, subject expertise, subject skills, effective participation in learning conversations, reflective learning and self-managing. These are the employ-ability skills that will create the flexible learners we need in the twenty-first century. Plan your collaborative projects to develop each of the PLTs then use the model in group work to assess how well they have developed the relevant skills.

What does Ofsted look for?

The questions below are from previous guidance for inspectors on evaluating teaching. They still provide a useful guide for considering progress in learning:

- What are the students actually learning as opposed to doing?
- Are they learning something new?
- Can all students make links between previous and new learning?
- Can the students talk about what they are learning or simply describe what they are doing?
- Do they produce work of a consistently good standard?
- Are they working independently?
- Are they self-reliant?
- How well do they collaborate?
- Do they show initiative?

Ensuring that *all* your students are making progress when they are working in groups is a key part of your planning and your intervention. This chapter aims to ensure that group work in your lessons demonstrates optimal collaboration for learning.

Remember: more group work means more active learning by the students and less talking by you.

'Students should have three times as much time doing stuff in lessons than you spend chatting at them.'

Beadle (2010)

How to form groups

Young people like to work with their friends and sometimes this works well, but on occasions it reinforces prejudices towards others and is too easy. Vary the groups so that students are challenged to work with a variety of different people and become conscious of the need to negotiate, mediate and facilitate each other's learning. Explain that working with a range of individuals may feel uncomfortable but this will make them more flexible and better communicators. Reinforce the 'unconditional support' ethos from Chapter 2 so that they strive to engage everyone in the group and ensure all are progressing.

'Whatever the activity or learning a class led discussion will never be as engaging as brilliantly engineered small group discussion ... It is in the setting of paired or grouped discussion work that you can mark yourself out as the kind of teacher who has thought properly about how learning works, and who is in possession of a special level of super-cool, advanced pedagogical skills.'

Beadle (2010)

'The campaign for self-discipline and collective responsibility is well worth the effort.'

Ginnis (2002)

For maximum flexibility and to extend teamworking skills, vary the groupings by using:

- Ability groups and sometimes mixed ability groups.
- Gender groups.
- PLTs groups (i.e. put all the skilled creative thinkers in one group or all the good teamworkers in another).
- Expert groups. If some students know more about the subject, group them together for a discussion then disseminate them across the other groups later.
- Friendship groups. Total choice or friendship pairs merged together.
- Random groups. Pull names out of a hat to surprise them.

For each group session make sure the students fill in a simple group- and self-assessment sheet that focuses on learning progress. For example:

How did our group do?	How did I do?
What did we learn? Even better if we ...	What did I learn? Even better if I ...

Chapter 5

Group dynamics

In the perfect lesson, the purpose and point of teamwork is to enhance the learning progress of *all* members of the group. It is important to tell students that it is normal for groups to go through challenges and disagreements and that this is when they learn how to improve their teamwork skills. Remember to teach the four stages of good group formation mentioned on page 25 (forming, storming, norming and performing), so that both students and teachers accept the need for teams to resolve problems themselves. Accept that storming will happen and fall outs will occur but that the students have to resolve this – and doing so will improve their communication skills and empathy. Teach how sports teams, quiz teams or army battalions succeed most when they work together. This will help to give an insight into the synergy that can be created in collaborative learning.

For an 'outstanding', students need to be highly considerate and very supportive of each other's learning in lessons.

An example of outstanding learning and teaching: BTEC Sport Year 10: soft tissue injuries (25 students)

- Lively, fun, active session referenced to clear lesson objectives.
- Very encouraging and supportive ethos.
- Genuine collaboration within groups.
- More-able students assessing and coaching others.
- Lesson builds well on previous learning with good understanding of technical terms allowing in-depth discussion of techniques.
- Teacher monitors understanding and development: listens, questions, explains, summarises.
- All students fully involved and making excellent progress.

Make the main aim of group work to enhance the learning and performance of each other. Imagine that your life depended on *all* of you doing well!

A culture of collaborative learning will help everyone accept the central goal (or norm) of the group: *We all need to make this work so that we can all learn as much as possible.* Quite often students get caught up in the drive towards the outcome rather than realising the power of the process.

If the main aim of the team is to produce the very best water rocket (see the collaborative activity on pages 28–29) then some of the group may dominate and take over. However, if you want *all* students to make progress then the group needs to be aware that everyone must know what is going on and contribute to making the rocket work. The team must be very clear about the outcomes required. For example, it could be 'the best rocket made by the best teamwork'; so a high quality outcome produced by just one member of the group would not be acceptable. This must be acknowledged in the success criteria.

Groups must have a set of rules that make it second nature to behave in certain ways as they work together. For example:

- We will all take turns to speak.
- We will all get the chance to speak.
- We will listen to each other when we speak.
- We will support each other's contributions and collectively prevent any negative comments.
- We will all help each other to learn as much as possible from this activity.
- We will all work hard to make our team successful.

What follows is an example of notes taken by an observer in a Year 9 science lesson where outstanding learning and teaching was seen in practical group work:

STUDENTS: Actively engaged in answering questions; peer review of their answers leads to well-focused discussion; students confident to query what the teacher has said; excellent planning and practical work in groups; all groups are working hard and making significant progress in understanding.

TEACHER: Enforces time limits; reviews early answers; targets questions well; circulates between groups and discusses understanding; organises smooth transition from planning to activity; stops lesson to highlight learning.

> Teaching each other is the most
> powerful way for young people to learn.

Group roles

Encouraging groups to allocate different responsibilities to different students will help the group work well and give the students a chance to reflect on how well they fulfilled the role. Roles within a team could include some or all of the following:

- Motivator
- Coach
- Scribe
- Clerk
- Leader
- Chairperson
- Finisher
- Completer
- Ideas generator
- Challenger
- Expert

Students can also both *evolve* and *revolve* – evolve roles for the group according to the task and activity and be encouraged to revolve the different responsibilities so they can practise various skills and develop flexibility. When teamwork is good, and this becomes routine, then students will be able to talk to an observer about their role, their learning within the group and how well it worked on this occasion and at other times in the past.

Leadership: the optimum skill for teacher and student

Leadership is about taking responsibility and being accountable for the outcomes. All students should have an opportunity to take the lead role on various occasions. Rewarding leaders for managing their team effectively so that *everyone* achieves a good learning outcome will be an important part of your lesson. Teach students about leadership and model effective teaching as leadership in the classroom.

Leadership can take various forms:

- *Quiet leadership* that leads from the background but gives the team confidence.
- *Inspiring leadership* that sets an example through hard work and taking risks.
- *Democratic leadership* that makes sure everyone has their say and feels part of the decisions made.
- *Determined leadership* that never gives up and ensures the job is done.

In the plenary for the lesson help students to consider:

- How did the leadership work in our group?
- What difference did it make to the outcome?
- How could it be better?

> The question asked at the end of BBC's
> *The Apprentice* is always: Was he or she a
> good leader? Good leaders don't get fired!

How do you know they are learning?

Mastering the management of really good collaborative learning is very challenging because the teacher must know how the team activity is progressing the learning for *all* students. You may need to intervene in the group work at key moments to consolidate the learning and demonstrate the progress. You can use a progress arrow or the Assessment of Pupil Progress (APP) progression model to aid the metacognition process by asking how far they have moved towards the learning outcome.

For example:

No idea	Some	Most	Got it!	I can explain the difference between solids and gases physically and at a molecular level.
	But I can explain what I do/do not get.		Ask me anything.	

The best way of measuring progress is to build some proper DIRT (Dedicated Improvement and Reflection Time) into the plenary at the end of all collaborative work.

Regularly reviewing what has been learned and how it has happened using the arrow method or any of the other methods described is the key to developing a routine and habit where students discuss and measure their own individual progress towards your tightly set differentiated objectives.

In this way your lesson is rigorous, adds value and (hopefully) demonstrates outstanding progress.

At the end of the lesson, the test of great collaborative learning will be for students to ask themselves:

- What did I learn in this lesson?
- How did my group help or hinder my learning?
- How much progress have I made in my subject's skills and knowledge?
- How much progress have I made with my teamworking skills?

You should consider how aware you are of the progress being made by all groups of students, particularly the progress of those with specific needs (the most able, the SEND child, the quiet boy, the disruptive girl, etc.). To ensure they are making progress will require well-crafted support to make for 'perfect' collaborative learning.

Now you just have to plan the next lesson ...

Top tips from teachers to develop leadership skills for students:

- Set up 'expert workshops' where certain pupils who are good at technology or literacy, for example, can share their expertise during a lesson.
- Create your own class version of Yellow Pages with a list of what each pupil is particularly good at and encourage the class to use this list when they are stuck and need help from someone 'who can'!
- Make sure every child has a chance to teach the class something. Plan it, deliver it and assess it! Teaching is the best way of learning – as we teachers know well. Use this method to deepen learning or introduce something new that one child already has skills or knowledge about e.g. using apps on your iPad, building a fire or conjugating verbs.

Chapter 6

Top tips for using human and other resources effectively to enhance progress in learning

The use of all the resources available to you to make the learning work is an important part of the perfect lesson. This is a huge area and this chapter provides just a selection of examples of good practice that may be helpful in ensuring you create a great lesson.

Resources, including new technology, must make a marked contribution to the quality of learning. The most expensive resource you have in your classroom though is another adult.

'Direct observations in lessons will be supplemented by a range of other evidence to enable inspectors to evaluate the impact that teachers and support assistants have on pupils' progress.'

Ofsted, *School inspection handbook* (2015): 45

Ask yourself: If you plan to use ICT or have learning support assistants or teaching assistants (TAs) in your lesson, how will they make a difference to the learning?

What follows are a few top tips for using TAs or any other adult in your classroom. For further information and expert advice see Phil Beadle's *How to Teach* and Jim Smith's *The Lazy Teacher's Handbook*.

- Ensure they have a copy of the lesson plan and make sure they are mentioned in it!
- Try to discuss it in advance with them and plan for them to take an active role.
- The active role can be within a group activity that may be enhanced by the presence of an adult. If you do this, make certain the TA is fully briefed about how to facilitate a group activity without taking it over.
- A section of the lesson can be delivered by the TA. This is particularly successful when they are confident and can include some of their own expertise or experience. For example, in a science lesson they could describe the impact of a wind farm near their home or in a maths lesson discuss the way they use functional maths skills at home. Often the TA will have knowledge from personal interests or study. Make sure you know about these and use them. Students love it when you vary the input.
- Use the TA to observe and record skills development with a small number of students for assessment purposes. This

is especially useful when groups are working together and you want to know how particular students with certain needs are performing in the group dialogue or activity. This can be followed up by an individual discussion with the student concerned as a support to the DIRT (Dedicated Improvement and Reflection Time).

- Use TAs to support students who have problems with English as a second language but remember to plan this in advance so that the TA has a list of the key words translated and you have agreed upon scaffolded tasks.

- If TAs are working with particular students, make sure they are not doing the work for them and ask them to report to you about the progress made by that student and the next steps that are needed.

Using ICT

Technology is such an integral part of the learning that it is sure to be built into your long-term schemes and plans. However it must be subject to the question: *How is it contributing to the progress in learning of the students?* Some of the best cross-curricular uses of ICT are listed below:

- Interactive games and quizzes that rehearse mental arithmetic or vocabulary.
- Student participation by voting for answers.
- Laptops for researching historical events.
- Showing films and clips as examples of narrative development.

- Students filming themselves to see skills development in PE and reflect on progress and next steps.
- Mobile phone text messages, emails, tweets and blogs used as a learning review to engage students in sharing what they have learned.
- Presenting learning to others.

There is no doubt that mobile technology, such as iPads, is revolutionising education. From age 3–18 the world of apps and social media, such as Twitter, are providing massive opportunities for learning in new and exciting ways. Coming to your classroom now are pupils who use such technology as easily as their right hands. Let them take the lead and teach you and the class what they know. For teachers this is an opportunity for modelling every mistake as a learning experience!

Other resources

Interesting resources can make a lesson engaging and impress any observer. Novelty engages the emotional brain – which explains why students always remember the lesson when you wore the horned helmet to discuss the Vikings. However, the resources must always contribute to, not distract from, the progress the students are making in learning.

In his useful checklist for what constitutes an outstanding lesson, Tim Hann (2010) when describing the use of resources said: 'Periods of teacher-led information are short. They use ingenious techniques and innovative aids and resources, directly facilitating student curiosity, query, engagement, and a desire to tackle the learning'.

Tony Thornley (2007) stated in an article, 'The teaching is exciting and interesting (for example, through use of stimulating resources or other adults in the lesson); it may be inspired, although it doesn't have to be'. Also, 'Students have easy access to, and make use of, additional resources which they use independently to support or enhance their learning'.

Some examples of resources that have worked well in lessons include:

- Powerful images, still or moving.
- Artefacts that are mysterious (like a closed box with something magic inside) or shocking (such as a real brain or lungs)
- Wigs or masks worn by the teacher or students.
- Toys such as soft balls, models, puppets and so on will grab the interest of the class no matter what their age. If they can contribute to the learning then they will certainly provide engaging activities.
- A real live expert on the subject – someone from the community who can tell a relevant story, a business expert or an ex-pupil will be a very impressive addition to your 'perfect' lesson.

A word of warning: wonderful resources are exciting and engaging but when planning your perfect lesson always remember to ask:

> How much do the resources contribute to the progress the students are making in learning?

Don't get distracted!

Chapter 7

Ofsted 2015: what it means for the perfect lesson

Since September 2012 schools have had to demonstrate excellent teaching and learning as 'typical' to gain an 'outstanding' grade. The quality of teaching and learning is now firmly a central focus for judgements. These judgements will focus on what children typically experience in your school that helps them make excellent progress towards their qualifications and future destinations. This means more classroom observation for more teachers, thus making this little book an even more important tool for every teacher in the classroom.

However, an important and welcome development from 2014 was the decision to no longer grade individual lessons, but to use the evidence gained in observations and from other sources to make an overall judgement on the quality of teaching across the whole school. This book has stressed that the quality of your teaching is not just about the observation on the day but what you deliver five hours a day, five days a week. Inspection teams will scrutinise work, talk to pupils and parents and look at the school's records of observation and performance management. They will track groups of pupils such as those who have special needs and see how they are being supported to make extra progress across different lessons. They will also look at how *all* pupils improve in literacy and maths in all lessons. The progress that *all* pupils make in each and every classroom will help schools to show 'continuous improvement' – no matter what the starting point.

There are four areas to reflect on in particular:

1. Closing the gap for the most vulnerable pupils. What percentage of your students make marked and demonstrable progress in a key stage?

2. Using assessment to ensure effective learning – every day and over time.

3. Teaching (and demanding) outstanding behaviours for learning on the day and demonstrating evidence of their impact over time.

4. Improving literacy in all subjects and phases – with teachers and TAs modelling Standard English and developing it with students every lesson.

Mind the gap: progress for all – and especially those that need it most!

The focus on good 'progress' and engaged, resilient, ambitious learners working independently in the classroom on challenging activities will still be the mark of an outstanding lesson. In addition, the 2015 framework has a particular focus on individuals and their progress.

'Inspection is primarily about evaluating how well individual children and learners benefit from the education provided by the school or provider. Inspection tests the school's or provider's response to individual needs by observing how well it helps all children and learners to make progress and fulfil their potential.'

Ofsted. *The common inspection framework* (2015): 6

There should also be high expectations of all, and in particular, vulnerable groups of students, such as British working class white boys, ethnic minorities or SEND students. Where Pupil Premium funding has been awarded for individuals or groups of disadvantaged children the gaps between outcomes for these pupils and national averages must be narrowing rapidly. You must be able to prove that the funding is making a difference to outcomes – however it is used. Governors also need to be aware of how this funding is used and whether it is effective.

Make sure you know where the *attainment gaps* in your school are and plan EVERY lesson to help these pupils make *extra* progress.

Part of the solution to this is to *use teaching assistants* (your most expensive classroom resource) more effectively to help these pupils progress and close the gap in attainment.

Top tips for improving the use of TAs. Ensure:

- They know and understand the objectives of the lesson – and how they relate to the children they are working with.
- You have planned for their input and made a note of this on your plan.
- They understand progression in your subject and what progress you hope for from your students.
- They have a way to feed back to you the successes and failures of the learning in that lesson – which is linked to the objectives.
- They can mark and set targets linked to progression and objectives for their students.
- They can help students to set success criteria and understand exactly what they need to do.
- They can assess and observe – giving the one-to-one feedback that really works.
- They believe they can make a difference to progress.
- They are your eyes and ears in terms of identifying progress problems and what *you* need to do next.

The use of assessment and feedback to support effective learning

Ensuring that teachers assess accurately and that the information from this is then used effectively to plan the next steps for each child is still a central judgement in the 2015 framework.

Self-directed learning and group work will be a large percentage of your 'perfect' lesson, so use this time systematically and effectively to check understanding with individual pupils. Make sure that your interventions and those of any other adults have a real impact on the quality of learning and progress.

Effective feedback that supports continuing progress has a massive impact on pupil outcomes and so is a crucial aspect of effective teaching. (See Higgins et al., *The Sutton Trust-Education Endowment Foundation Teaching and Learning Toolkit*, 2014.) Any feedback must be focused on exactly what the pupil has to do to make progress. Teachers must ask questions in the classroom that help the student to find new strategies when they get stuck and to relish the challenge of learning from their mistakes. Clearly focused advice about how to move forward must be evident in scrutinised books and oral feedback.

It is then vital that the pupils are seen to act on and respond to the feedback.

Great teaching will also involve training your students to give and take constructive criticism to support each other's progress. *There is clear evidence from research that children teaching and coaching one another aids progress for giver and receiver.* So give them the success criteria and let them assess each other's work and provide targets for improvement. Deliver your input then pair up students to re-teach it to each other to deepen learning. Do some of this peer teaching and learning every lesson – with or without an inspector present.

As the grade descriptors for outstanding teaching, learning and assessment say:

> ▓ Teachers check pupils' understanding systematically and effectively in lessons, offering clearly directed and timely support.
>
> ▓ Teachers provide pupils with incisive feedback, in line with the school's assessment policy, about what pupils can do to improve their knowledge, understanding and skills. The pupils use this feedback effectively.
>
> ▓ Pupils are eager to know how to improve their learning. They capitalise on opportunities to use feedback, written or oral, to improve.
>
> Ofsted, *School inspection handbook* (2015): 48–49

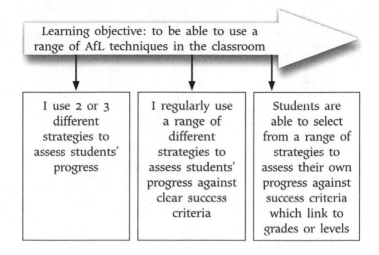

Subject progress

Ensure you (and your students) are very clear about the progression model in your subject. Use differentiated objectives to clarify how the learning journey may progress. Here is an example of how English teacher David Didau developed the continuum model in this book to help his students understand their starting points and where they need to go.

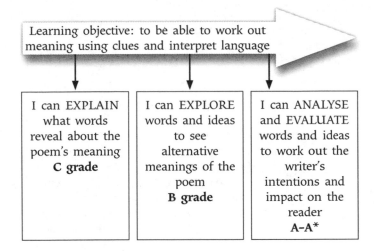

Note: Thanks to David Didau for his graphic examples of how we can use the continuum model exemplified in this book to see our learning and student learning as a journey.

Behaviour for learning: relentlessly nurture unconditional support for each other's learning and progress

Behaviour and attitude in the classroom and across the school is a very clear focus for any inspection. Teachers are expected to manage pupils' behaviour effectively through the consistent application of clear rules and curb any low-level disruption.

- Pupils' impeccable conduct reflects the school's effective strategies to promote high standards of behaviour. Pupils are self-disciplined. Incidences of low-level disruption are extremely rare.
- For individuals or groups with particular needs, there is sustained improvement in pupils' behaviour. Where standards of behaviour were already excellent, they have been maintained.

Ofsted, *School inspection handbook* (2015): 52

Pupils must be clear that they come to school to learn and to support the learning of others. There needs to be a high level of engagement, collaboration and cooperation. The very best schools have a culture of mutual peer support and pure enjoyment of the life of the school. When children attend this type of school they experience the mix of challenge and support that will make sure they fulfil their potential. There will be a tangible atmosphere in the playground, classroom and staffroom – that children and staff are proud to attend their school. It is possible to have a rigorous drive for academic standards alongside a culture of caring and sharing. I know because I have seen it and felt the 'buy in' of every pupil and teacher. It is driven by visionary leadership and relentless optimism, alongside lots of extra-curricular enrichment. If you haven't got this in your school, you can still have it in your classroom.

Planning engaging and challenging tasks that relate to the real world outside of school is the best way to ensure great behaviour. You will also need to establish a consistent approach to a classroom ethos that has zero tolerance to disruption of learning. The most powerful way to do this is to enlist the students themselves. The habits of behaviour that you establish will be obvious to any inspector. Be meticulous and monomaniacal about establishing kindness, confidence and a love of learning.

Top tips for improving behaviour and learning:

- Get students to create their own set of 'brilliant learning' laws that fit in with the school's behaviour policy but create a 'buy in' for your particular subject/context. Display prominently and remind often!

- Make 'supporting learning for all' a focus for reward and praise.

- Use football and other team analogies to show how working together makes us all winners.

- Explain that they all make more progress when they support each other.

- Say often 'I'm not going to give up on you' until the reluctant learners finally give in and get on with it.

For more on this see *Confident Classroom Leadership* by Peter Hook and Andy Vass.

Chapter 7

Literacy in your lesson

The concern about the lack of literacy and numeracy skills in young people (even those who get a 'C' grade in English at GCSE!) has been well rehearsed. As an English teacher passionate about communication skills for all, this development has my complete support. A single literacy coordinator in schools ensuring the subject 'key words' are up in every classroom will no longer suffice. Every teacher must make a contribution in every lesson to improving the literacy of pupils. Every opportunity to cross reference your subject with literacy or numeracy objectives should be taken if you are to be an excellent teacher.

> 'Inspectors will consider the impact of the teaching of literacy and the outcomes across the range of the school's provision. They will consider the extent to which the school intervenes to provide support for improving pupils' literacy, especially those pupils at risk of underachieving.'
>
> Ofsted, *School inspection handbook* (2015): 46

To start with, ensure that *your* literacy skills are *perfect* – check your spelling and grammar in every PowerPoint presentation or written word you place on the board or wall. Get into the habit of getting it right – *every time* (as an observer of lessons, I find at least 50 per cent of teachers make literacy errors). No excuses – you must model excellence. If you aren't confident, insist your school runs a course for teachers who need it.

The Perfect Lesson

Here are my top tips for making sure you do this for the 'perfect' lesson:

- Build literacy into your lesson plan.
- Introduce new vocabulary (not just subject related).
- Encourage reading aloud in class, paired and privately – value reading.
- Give wider subject reading suggestions, including relevant magazines.
- Make sure top tips on paragraph formation, spelling, punctuation and grammar are delivered as part of your input.
- Reward literacy skills used in your lessons.
- Encourage the use of the Standard English register, both spoken and written.
- Use texting, Twitter, email, etc. to emphasise good communication skills in your subject.
- Care about literacy skills in your lesson. Offer prizes for students who catch you out making a mistake and model mistakes as learning experiences.
- Remind students about writing in good clear sentences and paragraphs – if you show you value this, they will value it too.
- Look out for students who are not reading very much because others in the group are doing it for them.
- Mark spellings and give spelling tests for words in your subject.

■ Give students an opportunity to assess their writing skills using a simple grid whenever they do any written work. For example, see pages 59–62.

Teaching reading will be a focus for inspections in primary schools, including the delivery of synthetic phonics. Numeracy will also be a key aspect for primary schools. In secondary schools, the development of literacy will be expected in every subject. Delivering progress in literacy in your lesson will be expected if you are to be rated as 'outstanding'. This means you will have to draw attention to accurate spelling and well-formed sentences, as well as appropriate vocabulary that makes students' work effective. Up to Year 8, inspectors can listen to weaker readers and talk to them about how the school is helping them make progress. They will expect to see every teacher supporting the development of literacy skills in all lessons.

Finally, have you ever noticed that some students don't like to read and write? They are the very individuals who need to read and write more often in your lessons. More reading and writing is crucial for improvements in literacy.

Elect a literacy ambassador for your lesson and give that pupil the chance to check on the key words that would be useful to put in the class learning Rucksack or Treasure Chest. He or she might also try to catch you and others out on literacy or oracy errors so that the whole class can learn from them. A numeracy ambassador could have the challenge of finding a way to take the lesson content and make it into a real-life maths challenge.

The Perfect Lesson
quick checklist

Top tip: Inspectors will not expect teachers to prepare lesson plans for the inspection. However they will expect to see well planned lessons ...

Have you:

1. Set learning objectives that allow you to measure ☑
    progress for different groups. Are they clear,
    engaging and above all *owned* by the pupils?

2. Worked out exactly how you are going to measure ☑
    the impact of the learning in your lesson and build
    on it to demonstrate their progress?

3. Planned a lesson with a high proportion of active, ☑
    independent learning, choice and collaborative
    activity?

4. Built assessment as learning into your lesson so ☑
    that students can self- and peer-assess to monitor
    and demonstrate their own learning progress?

5. Identified various groups of students in your class and identified any special needs to ensure these groups make exceptional progress? ☑

6. Ensured your students have been taught how to work well together and give unconditional support for each other's learning? ☑

7. Addressed literacy/oracy/numeracy development in your lesson and modelled 'perfect' literacy yourself? ☑

8. Made sure students are really challenged in the activities and through the reflection? ☑

9. Planned to meet with any teaching assistant and discuss how they are going to contribute to student progress? ☑

10. Thought about how you are going to assess the progress in learning in plenaries or homework? ☑

And finally ... Don't forget to mentally rehearse it going brilliantly!

Good luck!

Postscript

And afterwards ...
feedback is the breakfast of champions

You will be observed teaching throughout your career and you can see this either as a threat or an opportunity. If you follow the advice given in this book, you can look forward to the opportunity to show off how you help your pupils make great progress.

Remember that it is possible in an inspection to be observed by two people, one of whom will be from your senior leadership team. When it is over, remember also that all teachers observed for more than 20 minutes are entitled to feedback – though not a grade.

Get that feedback, write it down and learn from it. Ask questions and be sure *you* know what you have learned from the experience and how to improve next time. Note down quotes so that you can remember exactly what was said. If you disagree with the judgements, say why and ask for clear development points to work on. There is more emphasis than ever on the observation leading to support and improvement and it not being an outcome in itself. If a member of your leadership team was present, request further feedback from them later. Remember ...

There is no such thing as failure – only feedback.

If you learn from the experience, lesson observations will be a very constructive part of your progression towards outstanding teaching. *All* teachers have had bad experiences in lesson observations. As was said in the introduction: *Most of the very best teachers have experienced an unsatisfactory judgement at some time in their careers. Learn from it, and it will work as a positive force in your development. Dwell on it, beat yourself up about it, argue about it, and it could be destructive and very demoralising.* It is in your school's interest to help you be the best teacher you can be.

In making a judgement on the effectiveness of leadership and management inspectors will consider:

- the effectiveness of the actions leaders take to secure and sustain improvements to teaching, learning and assessment and how effectively governors hold them to account for this

- how well leaders ensure that the school has a motivated, respected and effective teaching staff to deliver a high quality education for all pupils, and

---

how effectively governors hold them to account
for this
- the quality of continuing professional development
for teachers at the start and middle of their careers
and later, including to develop leadership capacity
and how leaders and governors use performance
management to promote effective practice across
the school

Ofsted, *School inspection handbook* (2015): 38

It's not just for Ofsted ...

Remember, an observation is only a brief snapshot of your
teaching. It could turn out to be like a flattering studio por-
trait or like that dire passport photo from one of those
booths! Either way it is just a snapshot. The aim of this book
is not simply to make that brief observation look outstanding
but for it to truly reflect your *everyday outstanding teaching*.

Lots of teachers can put on a flattering, made-up pose – but
it is difficult, if not impossible, for even the best of them to
magic outstanding lessons out of nowhere. The inspection
framework aims to discover the quality of the teaching that
is delivered every day of the year, not just during inspection.
The best way you can be 'outstanding' is to develop a flexible,
multifaceted approach that draws on the very best ideas and
which continually adapts and responds to individual learners'
needs. The evidence is that the very best teachers continually

self-evaluate and are relentlessly searching for ways to help their students improve their learning strategies.

There are lots of other great books available that offer advice on how to teach effectively; a brief list follows. For example, in my recent book *The (Practically) Perfect Teacher*, you can find out how the very best teachers continually work to improve their students' achievements. Read about and try out different strategies in your classroom. Make them your own by adapting them to suit your style and phase. Be the very best teacher you can be, every day and every lesson. That way anyone walking into your lesson will know you stand out!

References and further reading

Beadle, P. (2010). *How To Teach*. Carmarthen: Crown House Publishing.

Beere, J. (2013). *The (Practically) Perfect Teacher*. Carmarthen: Independent Thinking Press.

Beere, J. and Boyle, H. (2009). *The Competency Curriculum Toolkit: Developing the PLTS Framework through Themed Learning*. Carmarthen: Crown House Publishing.

Biggs, B. B. and Collis, K. F. (1982). *Evaluating the Quality of Learning: Structure of the Observed Learning Outcome Taxonomy*. Waltham, MA: Academic Press.

Black, P., Harrison, C., Lee, C., Marshall, B. and Wiliam, D. (2003). *Assessment for Learning: Putting it into Practice*. Buckingham: Open University Press.

Bloom, B. S. (1956). *Taxonomy of Educational Objectives, Handbook I: The Cognitive Domain*. New York: David McKay Co. Inc.

Crossland, J. (2010). Brain biology and learning. *School Science Review*, 337: 99–108.

Curran, A. (2008). *The Little Book of Big Stuff about the Brain.* Carmarthen: Crown House Publishing.

Dweck, C. S. (2006). *Mindset: The New Psychology of Success.* New York: Ballantine Books.

Farr, S. and Teach for America (2010). *Teaching as Leadership: The Highly Effective Teacher's Guide to Closing the Achievement Gap.* San Francisco: Jossey-Bass.

Gilbert, I. (2007). *The Little Book of Thunks.* Carmarthen: Crown House Publishing.

Gilbert, I. (2008). *The Book of Thunks.* Carmarthen: Crown House Publishing.

Ginnis, P. (2002). *The Teacher's Toolkit.* Carmarthen: Crown House Publishing.

Hann, T. (2010). You've Been Framed. *Leader* (published by the Association of School and College Leaders), issue no. 50. Available at: http://www.leadermagazine.co.uk/archive/.

Hargreaves, D. (chair) (2005). *About Learning: Report of the Learning Working Group.* London: Demos. Available at: http://www.demos.co.uk/files/About_learning.pdf?

Hattie, J. (2012). *Visible Learning for Teachers: Maximizing Impact on Learning.* London: Routledge.

Higgins, S., Katsipataki, M., Kokotsaki, D., Coleman, R., Major, L. E. and Coe, R. (2014). *The Sutton Trust-Education Endowment Foundation Teaching and Learning Toolkit.* London:

Education Endowment Foundation. Available at: http://www.suttontrust.com/about-us/education-endowment-foundation/teaching-learning-toolkit/.

Hook, P. and Vass, A. (2000). *Confident Classroom Leadership*. London: David Fulton.

Jackson, N. (2009). *The Little Book of Music for the Classroom: Using Music to Improve Memory, Motivation, Learning and Creativity*. Carmarthen: Crown House Publishing.

Ofsted (2009). *Twelve outstanding secondary schools: Excelling against the odds*. Ref. 080240. Available at: http://webarchive.nationalarchives.gov.uk/20141124154759/http://www.ofsted.gov.uk/resources/twelve-outstanding-secondary-schools-excelling-against-odds.

Ofsted (2015). *School inspection handbook*. Ref. 150066. Available at: https://www.gov.uk/government/publications/school-inspection-handbook-from-september-2015.

Ofsted (2015). *The common inspection framework: education, skills and early years*. Ref. 150065. Available at: https://www.gov.uk/government/publications/common-inspection-framework-education-skills-and-early-years-from-september-2015.

Rowe, J. (2007). My top ten tips: Assessment for learning. *Secondary Teachers Magazine*, July 2007. Available at: http://ia201120.eu.archive.org/tna/20090318011029/teachernet.gov.uk/teachers/issue51/secondary/features/mytop10tips assessmentforlearning/.

Smith, J. (2010). *The Lazy Teacher's Handbook: How Your Students Learn More When You Teach Less.* Carmarthen: Crown House Publishing.

Thornley, T. (2007). Make it Outstanding. *Leader* (published by the Association of School and College Leaders), issue no. 19. Available at: http://www.leadermagazine.co.uk/archive/.

Tuckman, B. (1965). Developmental sequence in small groups. *Psychological Bulletin,* 63(6): 384–399.

Wall, K., Hall, E., Baumfield, V., Higgins, S., Rafferty, V., Remedios, R., Thomas, U., Tiplady, L., Towler C. and Woolner, P. (2011). *L2L in Schools and FE Research Project.* London: Campaign for Learning.

Wiliam, D. and Black, P. (2006). *Inside the Black Box: Raising Standards through Classroom Assessment.* London: NFER Nelson. Available at: http://weaeducation.typepad.co.uk/files/black-box-1.pdf.

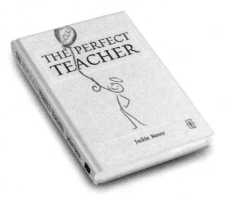

978-178135100-0

www.independentthinkingpress.com